THE ADOPTIVE PARENT TOOLBOX

INSIGHTS AND STORIES
FOR THE JOURNEY

Mike and Kristin Berry

Lulu Publishing Services rev. date: 2/2/2016

CONTENTS

FORWARD

An Unexpected Journey

In the frigid winter of 1998 I (Kristin) found myself filled with the warmth of new love. We locked eyes across the lobby of the boys' dorm at Cincinnati Christian University. I looked away pretending not to be interested. No more than a minute later he had made his way over to introduce himself. We spent the next few months inseparable. We agreed on almost all of life's greatest philosophies. (Which coffee shop in Cincinnati has the best coffee...) you know, the important stuff. Until the day I said I wanted to adopt.

The easy, free-flowing, conversation came to a halting stop. My beloved just looked at me with confusion. I came from an adoptive family, so I had never had a second thought about adopting. It was the very nature of my family's DNA. My youngest brother is adopted from Bulgaria, my aunt placed her baby for adoption when she was young, my grandmother was adopted by an aunt and uncle, and my grandfather grew up in the foster care system in the early 1900's. It was something I had always known I would do. However, here we were at an impasse. We saw each other in the new light of disagreement. I left the conversation that day without the rosy glow of blind love. We eventually decided that we made a good pair and got married in the summer of 1999. We put the discussion of children on the back burner and enjoyed our time alone as a couple for three years.

When the subject of family came up again, I followed the advice of a wiser, older woman (my mother) and began to pray for my own heart and the heart of my husband. I committed not to nag or pressure him. I prayed for my own heart to be clear on our path and for his mind to feel peace about how we would become a family as well. Over the next few months, a couple of things took place. He read an article in a magazine about a well-known musician whom he admired, Steven Curtis Chapman. Chapman, at the time, had just adopted a child from China. Then my husband met a friend for lunch who had adopted two older children. Lastly, a couple from church chatted with us between services about the adoption of their two beautiful little girls. Without so much as a word from me, his heart had been changed and my heart was at peace.

We began the paperwork at our local adoption agency and brought home our first infant daughter a whopping 2 months later! At the same time, a girl from our youth group began to spend more and more time with our family as her mom became increasingly ill. She was a wonderful "big sister" to our daughter and later officially became the big sister when we adopted her as an adult after her mother passed away. Two years later, another friend of ours found herself in some trouble and lost her two children into the foster care system. We scrambled to get our foster license and brought the two children home in less than three months. Their adoption was finalized 4 years later. Once a family has their foster license, there is never a shortage of placements. Over the next 9 years, 21 children would walk through our doors. We formed lifelong relationships with the children and their birth families. By the time we closed out our foster license, we had adopted 6 more children.

Never would we have believed this journey would be the landmark of our entire life. We both like order and uniformity. As first-born children, surrender does not come easy for either one of us. We each had a plan for how our life would go; little did we know that God had completely different plans for us. God was writing a pretty amazing story through the family we would eventually have. We often joke about how we could never have written a better script for our journey.

Unexpected? Yes. Difficult? For sure. Beautiful? Absolutely!

INTRODUCTION

How To Use This Toolbox

Before we go one step further in this book, we want to tell you *congratulations*. This may not be something you hear from family or friends for a while. They may take some time to warm up to the idea of adoption. So, we will tell you- *Congratulations!* Adoption is such an amazing journey and we know that your family will be blessed. It won't always be an easy journey, and unfortunately, the road will not always rise to meet you. No matter what happens, it's worth it.

It's probably safe to say that since you purchased a book called **The Adoptive Parent's Toolbox**, you have an interest in adoption. Hopefully this book will encourage you on your path or inspire you to begin the journey of adoption. It was created with *you* in mind. Almost 13 years ago we were in your shoes, just starting out, trying to find our way, and wondering (just a little) what in the world we had gotten ourselves into. We want to provide you with the tools we wish we'd had when we started down this road.

Start by Picturing a Real Toolbox

The best place to begin is to picture this book like it's an actual toolbox that you keep in your home. A typical toolbox will be filled with a hammer, various screwdrivers, a level, a chisel, maybe a cordless drill, a tape measure, a knife or two, a socket-wrench set, crescent wrench, chalk-line, some pencils, a stud-finder (my personal favorite), and much more. Here is what I find interesting about my toolbox. All of the tools in it are useful for something, but not all are necessary for everything. The same is true for adoption and this toolbox. Just like you would use a hammer and nail to hang a picture and not a crescent wrench, some of you will read through this and discover that not every tool we list for the journey will be necessary for you. That's okay. If you find yourself looking through these pages and skipping some of the chapters because they don't apply, no problem! Skip them. Only pull the tools out that you need. Leave the others in the *box*. To help you navigate to the right tool we've organized this book into 3 sections. Section 1 is for pre-adoptive parents and centers on expectations and preparation. Section 2 covers the post-adoption ins and outs. The final section, Section 3, is a list of some of the best resources we know of on adoption.

One last thing before we move on, we want you to know something very important. You will meet many professionals along your journey. They may have the book knowledge but lack the experience. Some will be helpful some will not. We don't have PhD's. What we do have, is real life experience. That's the perspective that this toolbox is written from. Nearly 100% of this book has been birthed from personal experience. We believe there is great power in personal experience and sharing, openly, the stories of our life. There's power found in having several tools at your disposal. If I wanted to build a house but all I had was a hammer, I wouldn't get very far. If I had to nail two pieces of wood together but all I had was a screwdriver, it just wouldn't work. However, if I have an entire toolbox, I would be in business. We are writing this out of what we like to call the "been-there, done-that, wished-we-would've-known" place.

No amount of preparation will circumvent the detours, bumps, bruises and downright painful experiences you are guaranteed to have on this journey. Sometimes it's easy to go into adoption with eyes partially closed. This leads to disappointment and bewilderment when things begin to lose their rosy glow. If that's where you are right now, we encourage you to open your eyes. We are sharing some tough experiences with you so that you may find strength in the truth. So...ready to get started? Great! We are too. Here we go.....

CHAPTER 1

Well Known But Widely Misunderstood

Wow! You've purchased this book because you've decided to go on the adoption journey. That's pretty awesome. Kudos to you. But *get ready!* You are about to venture into a world that will react oddly to your decision. We faced this 13 years ago. People questioned our decision, looked at us strangely, and asked the ever-insulting question, "Can't you have kids of your own?" We were quite the spectacle because our family was now multi-racial. I (Mike) will never forget being at a family gathering and fielding questions over my daughter's race. Some family members and acquaintances just couldn't see the same thing that we saw, a daughter.

Regardless of the type of adoption you choose, you will have those who hurt you out of ignorance. Adoption is a well-known thing in our culture. Ask anyone walking down the street about adoption and there's a 90% likelihood they'll tell you something factual about adoption. Adoption has been featured in movies, television shows, talk-shows, and even glorified through the lives of A-list actors and actresses in Hollywood. There have been books and magazine articles written on the subject, and even entire blogs (your's truly) dedicated to the subject.

One thing I do want to make extremely clear is that you will never, ever, ever be fully prepared for any and all situations you experience in adoption. In-spite of all the hours you put into researching adoption online, reading articles, talking to other adoptive families, you still may encounter some curveballs. Some friends of ours went into their international adoption experience budgeting $50,000 and expecting 2 children. They ended up spending $105,000 and bringing home 3. We thought we'd have 4 or 5, we have 8. We would've told you 10 years ago that there was no way we could raise children with extreme trauma or fetal alcohol spectrum disorder. We're raising several.

For all of the knowledge the world has on adoption, it's still widely misunderstood. We live smack dab in the middle of a world that is familiar with adoption, but disconnected from the reality of it. Don't believe me? How many stores like Target, Walmart or Kohl's have an adoption registry? Most have a general baby registry but on the first page it asks for the mother's due date. No place to register for a child who is expected with no set arrival date, no place to register for a child who is 2, 5, 16. Those stores didn't do that to discriminate, they just lack the knowledge.

The best defense is a good offense, or something like that. If you know what you are about to walk in to, you will be better prepared. It's our goal to prepare you for many possible scenarios as we can.

By now you're probably reading this wondering, "Well, how do we handle the reality that many in our circle of friends or family will misunderstand our decision?" Great question! The best answer is, keep your head up, and be confident of your decision to adopt, regardless of what others say or think. Someone will always have an opinion. Even your own mother might be critical. Ignore it. Don't listen to it. This is your life. You were meant to adopt! Repeat that last sentence to yourself- "You...Were...Meant...To...Adopt!" Keep repeating that over and over, especially when the naysayers, the critics, and the haters start barking at you!

When we first adopted, we realized that others just didn't "get it." As tough as it was, we had to stay focused. We had to be okay with being "weird." Today, we're glad we did. What we didn't realize all those years ago was that our family would go on to impact several other families, and influence their decision to adopt.

Unanswered Questions

If anyone misunderstood adoption it was me (Mike). In fact, I would describe me as clueless. I had heard of adoption, was familiar (a little) with what it was all about, but I was really clueless as to why a family would choose to adopt or what the intention behind it was.

When we began the journey, we both really had no idea where to begin. We were clueless as to what type of adoption was right for us, or even who to call with questions. Can anyone relate? We decided to adopt internationally at first, because Kristin's brother was adopted from Bulgaria and we figured "International" was just what everyone did when they adopted. Yep....clueless.

Actually, Kristin was focused, and clued in much quicker than I did. She did her homework. All of it, even down to the tiniest penny we would spend on this whole thing. I, on the other hand, continued on in my lost state. I came from a family that didn't adopt. It's not that we were against adoption, it just wasn't what the Berry family did to build a family. Every child came into the world the old-fashioned way. In fact, if you could step back in time to 1993 or 1994 and have a conversation with the high school version of me, you would discover that I had a very specific path in mind for how this whole marriage and family thing was going to go. I would have told you that I was going to end up at a prestigious college in Cincinnati (where I was from), start dating a pretty blonde-haired, blue-eyed girl during my sophomore or junior year, get married the summer after college, and start making mini-me's and she's for the first decade or so of our marriage. Oh, and we were going to live in a medium-sized suburban home and drive two nice cars.

I had the blonde-haired, blue-eyed, married-the-summer-after-college thing right. I even had the time frame for dating right. We met in the middle of my junior year of college. Child-Rearing on the other hand, went very different from what I had "planned."

I remember the night clearly. The year was 1998. It was December, it was cold, and the wind was howling (not blowing), but howling over the edge of the West Cincinnati hills where Cincinnati Christian University (then Cincinnati Bible College) is located. We sat in my 1992 metallic blue Pontiac Firebird, trying to stay warm, in a parking space next to the campus library, talking, after a night out on the town. There may have even been a snow flurry or two swirling around. Did I mention it was cold? Frigid to be exact.

That night will forever be etched in our memory because that was the night when our adoption journey began. However, it didn't start off very "rosy." As we drove back to campus the topic of marriage (we were already engaged), and parenting came up. What began as a discussion, ended in a pretty heated disagreement. At one point, Kristin looked at me and said, "I want to adopt all of our children!"

"Umm, what?" I replied.

"You heard me," Kristin said, "Adopt...our children...all of them!"

"Yeah, I heard you, but I don't think I'm believing you," I replied.

"I want to adopt our children," Kristin reiterated.

"Okay, okay, okay, wait a minute," I started to rant. "There's one thing you need to know about the Berry family. We all grow up, we go to college, we meet a nice girl or boy, we get married, and then we make mini-me's of the two of us. It's pretty awesome!"

"But that's not the way you and I are going to do it."

As I mentioned earlier, 'not against adoption, just clueless as to what it was really all about.' Fortunately, my heart changed and so did my perspective. We got married in July of 1999, and a pretty adventurous story unfolded. I'm grateful for a wife, friend and partner who patiently waited for me to see the beauty that she already knew and believed with adoption. I finally came around through a few years of prayer and the counsel of some good friends. Even though our end result turned out to be a good one, it wasn't void of questions, or fear, or worry. In 2002 when we were selected by a birth mother to adopt her baby, confusion and fear were common threads.

As we started out some really big questions came into play and, at times, held us hostage. Questions like "How are we ever going to pay for this?" "Who can we lean on? Who will understand this?"

Adoption can be a scary and overwhelming thing when you first begin. There are more questions than answers, it seems. Where do you begin? Who do you work with? Where do you find help? Do you go with an agency or respond to an ad in the newspaper? Should you adopt domestically, internationally or through foster care? What about this whole home study thing? How much does adoption cost? How do you find a good attorney who is reputable and honest? This is not to mention personal fears like, 'Will I be able to love a child I didn't give birth to?' or 'How do I share my child with their birth parent?' The list goes on and on.

Can I share some comforting news? We completely understand. We've been down this road and we've had these questions, and probably a few that you haven't thought of. You're not alone. Our heart is to come alongside of you and let you know that we're in your corner and we believe in you. The following pages of this book will answer some common questions pre-adoptive parents have in regards to home-studies, creating bios, the cost of adoption, the legal side, sharing your child's story, how to overcome loss, and more.

Our hope is that you find this to be encouraging and helpful. If nothing else, may the stories and experiences we share brighten your day and motivate you. May you understand that we are no different than you. When we first began we felt lost and alone. We're writing this because we don't want you to feel that way. You were meant to adopt. You wouldn't be reading this book if that weren't true.

Let me encourage you with this one truth- you are a future-shaper. Choosing to adopt means you are reshaping the future. When the process is becoming long and frustrating; when paper work gets lost or a birth mother changes her mind, remember this about yourself. When you are wondering if you will ever have the chance to be a mommy or daddy, find peace in knowing that God has a plan for you that you cannot see or understand. Rest in knowing that there will come a day where your questions will be answered and the child that you are supposed to raise will find his or her way to your home!

CHAPTER 2

Choosing An Outlet

Now that we've walked through some of the questions and the misunderstandings surrounding adoption, let's talk about first steps and where you begin.

This can be daunting at first. It was for us. In this high-tech digital, social media saturated world, there seems to be so many avenues. Before you even begin the process you can become overwhelmed- "Do I work with an agency or respond to the want ad I saw in our local newspaper?" "Should we adopt domestically or internationally?" "What about foster-to-adopt? I've heard that involves little cost but can take years!" Which outlet is the best for you? This is undoubtedly the biggest series of questions that people have when they begin the process. As we talked about in the introduction of this book, we just sort of figured that international adoption is what everyone did since Kristin's parents adopted her brother from Bulgaria, and everyone we had ever talked to about adoption seemed to have adopted from China, or Russia, or Guatemala. We had this assumption because we hadn't known anyone who had gone through any other form of adoption.

We had heard of domestic adoption but never considered it. We were familiar with foster-to-adopt from movies or news stories we would hear. We really had no idea where to start. Fortunately, as we were working through our home study to adopt internationally, a woman from Adoption Support Center in Indianapolis, Indiana asked us matter-of-factly why we were choosing international. When we gave her our "Isn't that what you do" answer she smiled and shared the facts about domestic adoption with us. The rest, as they say, is history! Let's begin with agencies verses want ads, and independent websites.

Never, _ever_ choose to adopt through a want-ad in your local newspaper or through a website you stumble across on Craigslist randomly on the internet. These are loaded with fraud. Even those who are recommended by credible sources. Don't trust them. In fact, run from them. Each year thousands of stories litter the headlines of newspapers detailing the heartbreak of an excited couple, who were ready to adopt, but found themselves swindled out of thousands of dollars because they hastily responded to an ad in their newspaper of a person claiming to handle adoption processes. The angle of many con-artists is to prey upon hurting and expectant couples. They tap into the high emotion or the feelings of loss that many couples go through.

Choose an adoption agency instead. Ask around for recommendations from people you respect. Interview the agency. Set up an appointment and ask as many questions as you can think of. Work diligently to find the agency that matches your personality, beliefs and needs.

CHAPTER 3

Creating A Bio That's Unforgettable

One of the most important things you will do during the pre-adoptive process is create a family biography (bio for short). A bio is simply the document, or packet, you create to advertise yourself and your family to birth parents. It contains pictures, information on who you are, why you want to adopt, tidbits about your family, what you do for a living, what your family make-up is like, what kind of home you live in, and more. If you are using a private agency, this is the document they will use to promote you and your family to prospective birth parents who are placing their child for adoption. Bottom line, you want this to be amazing! Actually, you want it to be *beyond amazing*. This is one of several things you will want to invest lots of time and energy into.

Have you ever watched the Super Bowl? If not the game, at least the commercials? Many people actually watch the big game just to see the great commercials. And then, they talk about the most memorable ones to their friends in the office the next day. The commercials are such an important part of the Super Bowl, there are actual talk shows and morning radio shows that dedicate time, or entire shows, the following day, to analyze and talk about the commercials. Ad companies pay millions for just 20-30 seconds of airtime. Picture your pre-adoptive bio like one of the most memorable commercials from the Super Bowl. Something so great that others talk about it, rave over it, and hold you in high regard.

On February 2, 2002, just a little more than 4 months after our nation was attacked by terrorists on September 11, 2001,

Budweiser aired a commercial that will be forever remembered in history. The commercial depicted their signature Clydesdale horse-drawn wagon traveling across the Brooklyn Bridge, through some countryside, and stopping in a New Jersey field. Then, with the city and the Statue of Liberty in the background, the horses lower their heads, and bow. The screen fades to black and the caption "We'll Never Forget" appears. The commercial aired once, during that Superbowl only, and never again after. But, it's recognized as one of the most highly effective advertisements of all time!

Why?

Well, for starters, it was memorable. Second, it was authentic. And third, it was inspiring. No one really cared that it was an advertisement for a brewing company. What mattered was that it moved hearts in a time of high emotion and heartbreak in our nation.

Memorable, authentic, and inspiring. Let's break those three words down a little more.

Memorable.

Your bio needs to be so good that it doesn't leave the mind of a prospective birth mother (or father). Make it so compelling that they simply can't get you out of their mind or heart after looking through bios. Tell your story. Share your hurts, your longings, your passions and hopes, but make it memorable.

Authentic.

Be yourself. Don't copy any other bio or anything you've seen out there. The agency will have a format (or they will actually put the components together), but you will have say so over the content they use. It will be yours to submit. Create a bio that is purely you. Don't copy something someone else has already done. Be honest. If you have a lot of kids already, say that. In fact, be proud of that. If you live in a rural part of town, don't pretend you're in a thriving community. There is a birth-family looking for exactly what you have to offer. Be yourself.

Utilize the resources you have right under your own roof. When we put our bio together, we actually had a family member walk around with us and take pictures of us with our two dogs, out in our yard, taking a walk, reading books in a local bookstore, and sipping coffee at Starbucks. Even though the pictures were a little staged, they captured us in our natural surroundings.

Inspiring.

When we first went through the adoption process we had no kids, lived in a little farm house in Indiana, and had two dogs. Our house was small and adorable (Kristin's words). We had pictures from the fall when we bought the home and all of the leaves were multi-colored and beautiful. The house looked like something out of a Better Homes and Garden magazine. We also both served as the children's minister and student minister for a small church in central Indiana. We have always had a heart for children and students. In our bio, we talked a lot about that love, and our enthusiasm for the ministries we led. We highlighted our work in the church because it was important to us and it was also inspiring.

You may be thinking- "I don't really do anything inspiring!" This simply isn't true, if you take a hard look at your life, there are moments or experiences you've had that are inspiring. Serving in a local food pantry, visiting elderly neighbors, volunteering at the library or Boys and Girls club. Share your love for children. Share your dreams for your future family. Share what moves your heart and gets you up in the morning. Just tell your story. I promise, you'll move hearts.

Like A Used-Car Salesmen!

This is the moment where you begin to ask questions that are building up in your mind. "Yeah, but isn't this whole bio thing a little gimmicky and sales-pitchy?" It's not a gimmick, because this isn't the Home-Shopping Network! It's not Black Friday either. This is real life. Real people have walked into an agency and indicated that they want to (or need to) place their unborn child in the care of people who will raise them with love and support. You are advertising your family. The balance will be in doing it authentically.

Remember Their Emotions.

Earlier, as I (Mike) wrote about the Budweiser commercial that aired during the Super Bowl in 2002, I said that what mattered most was that it moved hearts and inspired people during a time of heartbreak and high emotion. The people who were impacted personally still get choked up when talking about it. It cut so deep into their lives that the wound will probably always be a little open. They knew they had to move on with their life because there was really no other choice. The commercial impacted people because it was a real expression of emotion.

Birth parents are going to experience high emotions and heartbreak when they walk into an agency to place their child for adoption. As you put your bio together, and shed hopeful tears for the child you will one day bring home, remember the emotions of prospective birth parents reading it. You want them to know, in the midst of their grief, that the child they willingly placed in your arms will be well-taken care of. You want them to know that you are real too and that you feel for them and the difficult decision they are making.

Picturing Their Child With You.

You want your perspective birth mother (or birth parents) to walk out of the agency, after looking at your bio, with a vision of what it will be like for their child to grow up in your home. You want her to picture their child's life with you.

One of the reasons our first daughter's birth mother chose us, was that she knew, by looking at our pictures, and reading a little about us, that her child would be raised in a loving home. She saw pictures of us playing with our dogs, taking walks, spending time together, and living in our house. We did everything in our power to show her, even briefly through pictures, what life in the Berry household was like. She also had things in common with us. She was born the same day as Kristin and ran track in high school just like Kristin did. She loved that we were both serving in a church and thought our home was adorable.

Adoption Bio Checklist.

Here's a brief checklist to use as you create your bio.

Content:
- A current about page.
- A list of hobbies.
- A paragraph about your profession (can also be a hobby)
- A paragraph about the members of your family.
- A compelling *Why* section detailing why you've chosen to adopt.
- A paragraph about your support community (talk about family who are close or friends who will be surrounding you and supporting you).

Pictures:
- 5-10 snapshots in your natural environment (at home, at your favorite coffee shop, your town's park, etc.)
- Up to 5 professional photos (one for the cover of your bio, the rest placed throughout the bio).
- 1 picture of the front of your house.
- 1 or 2 of the interior.
- 1 or 2 of your family altogether.
- Several of your house (snapshots), even the room where your child will sleep.
- A few photos of your pets, your church, your country club, or favorite restaurant (you want to capture the places where you live). **These can also be snapshots.

One word of caution: make sure that none of the pictures or content you include in your bio contains personal information like phone numbers, license plate numbers, or any part of your address. It's also a good idea for you to take generic pictures of the places you frequent like Starbucks, a park, or a location in your hometown. Most adoption agencies will have guidelines or restrictions for this as well.

Pay Attention To Detail.

One thing that we didn't even realize when we did our very first bio was that, in several snapshots of us, I was wearing a sweatshirt that had the logo of a local high school in our area imprinted on it. The agency we were working with didn't catch it either. Fortunately, we lived in a separate town from the high school so it really wasn't an issue. We weren't in any danger, and chances are you and your family won't be either, but it's always a good thing to be detailed. The last bit of information I will leave you with is that, if you go with a trusted agency, they will most likely have their own set of guidelines for your bio. Go with their's and use this chapter as a reference.

Are you getting excited? You should be! You are one step closer once the bio is done.

CHAPTER 4

Paperwork Mountain

Adoption requires a lot of paperwork and it will take a long time. You will be frustrated. You will probably swear...*a lot*. You may get into a verbal fight with random people because you're so frustrated. Okay, just kidding. Perhaps you will just want to quit. Don't quit. It's worth it. We promise!

I (Mike) hate filling out paperwork. I also hate to read directions or lengthy pages that explain how to fill out paperwork. Kind of ironic that an author hates to do this, right?

Recently, we purchased a new air conditioner for my daughter's bedroom and it came with a lot of instructions and a lot of paperwork. I nearly came unglued. Okay, perhaps that's a bit dramatic. But I was frustrated. In my mind, I wanted a quick solution. I needed an "Easy Button" for the air conditioner assembly. Really, who doesn't want an Easy Button when it comes to assembling anything.

The adoption process is no stranger to paperwork. Lots of paperwork to be exact. If you are adopting internationally be prepared to write a book. Paperwork comes with the territory and it can be overwhelming and defeating. However, it's important and it allows for every detail of the process to be covered. The biggest question we get from pre-adoptive families is, "How?" *How* will we get this completed in time? *How* can we climb this mountain? *How* will we get through this?

The answer is not all that profound. You take it *one* step at a time. That's it. There's no magic formula. You must place one foot in front of the other. I know how it is to stare at a stack of papers from a case manager, or a packet your adoption agency hands to you, and feel as if there's no way you'll get through it. To me, it's very similar to writing a book. Each time I set out to write a new book, including the manuscript for a novel I wrote several years ago, I felt overwhelmed. I literally had moments when I sat in my home office, staring at my computer screen, watching the curser blink on a blank page, feeling like I could never accomplish the goal of writing a book. In fact, even with this book, it took us months to really get started. All because of that little bug we all come down with called "being overwhelmed."

Do you know how we overcame that with this book, and lots of other projects we've set out to create?

We started.

That's right, we literally started typing, and typing, and typing. Pretty soon that typing led to more typing, and more typing, and more typing, until we woke up and had more than 20 chapters written and nearly 30,000 words on a page. The same principle is true for filling out paperwork. You must start. That's the first, and most powerful thing you can do in accomplishing your goal of getting through it. Start!

The second principle is just as simple as starting: Keep going!

Stay focused, stay consistent, and keep on writing and writing until each line on every page is filled in. Remember, one foot in front of the other. After you've started, and you keep going, the third thing you must do is not quit. It's easy to want to quit. In fact, in the middle of everything you have to compile, the photographs you must take, the family history you have to work through, the proof of income you have to submit, and on and on, you will have "quitter" moments. But as I said in the first paragraph of this chapter- don't quit! It's worth it. And, before you know it, you will be done. That's what happened to us each time we set out to fill out the mountain of paperwork before us. We kept going, even though it was hard and we were distracted. Then suddenly, we were done.

- Start.
- Keep going.
- Don't quit.

Apply these three steps and you will find success. You will make it. We know because we have. Even when we couldn't find the focus, nor the strength to get our paperwork completed, we did. You can too!

CHAPTER 5

The Types & The Cost

By now you have probably realized you have more questions than answers when it comes to this whole adoption journey. We understand. Even after more than a decade of being adoptive parents, there are still questions we have. One of the things that Pre-Adoptive families tend to wrestle over first and foremost are the different types. Domestic? Or international? Over the past decade we have befriended several families who've adopted domestically, internationally, privately, publicly, and through the foster care system. There are some significant differences between each. Let's spend some time on them:

Domestic Adoption.

This is any adoption that takes places within the country you live in. This process is usually faster than international adoption or foster-to-adopt, averaging anywhere from 4-12 months from the beginning of the process to placement. Children are usually placed at birth. The average cost for this option is currently $17,000-$25,000 if you work with an agency. You can expect this to include birth mother living expenses, home study fees, lawyer costs and advertising. Working with an agency affords you the peace of mind that someone will walk alongside your family from start to finish. Some agencies also offer post-adoption counseling for adoptees, parents and birth-parents. Working with an adoption agency will also allow your family to meet on neutral ground or communicate through a mediator when needed. Our family adopted once through an agency. They were helpful and knowledgeable. We were able to focus on the joy of welcoming our new daughter home without worrying about the legal details.

Some families choose to work just with a lawyer to cut the cost of working with an agency. This option can be ideal if you already have an established relationship with the birth family. We adopted our oldest daughter using just a lawyer but our risk with this adoption was very low. All parties agreed to the adoption. Her birth mother and father had passed away years earlier and she was over 18. She consented to her own adoption. The lawyer helped us through all of the technicalities and took the guess work out of the process. Her adoption day was filled with excitement and happiness over the decision we had all made together.

International Adoption.

This is any adoption that takes place outside of the country you live in. The most well-known countries that families adopt from are China, Russia, and the Ukraine. However, there are many other countries that are open to this process. The average cost is around $25,000-$50,000, which goes toward travel expenses, various agency fees, specific country expenses, home study costs, and travel. On average, it can take anywhere from 12 months to 4 years. Each country is different when it comes to the types and ages of children that are available for adoption.

Foster-To-Adopt.

This is any adoption that happens as a result of working with the foster care system. Couples or families who choose this option must go through foster care training and then indicate their desire to be a foster-to-adopt home. This option can be a very long and drawn out process. On average it takes anywhere from 2-4 years to finalize an adoption. The good news? There is little, to no, costs associated with this option.

We are often asked by couples beginning the adoption journey, if this is the best option and what advice we would offer if so. Our answer is, "Yes," and "That depends on you!" We say yes because that's how the majority of our family was formed. Out of our 8 children, only 2 were adopted from private agencies. Everyone else came to us through foster care. Needless to say, we have a heart for foster care and foster-to-adopt. Plus, as I (Mike) have already mentioned, there are virtually no costs involved. Your state usually picks up the tab. That's great news If you are a low-income family or serve in ministry or another non-profit organization.

When we say, "It depends on you," what we really mean is, "Are you ready?" Ready for the rocky road ahead, ready for a long and drawn out process, ready to board a seemingly un-ending roller coaster ride, ready to spend many many days frustrated? I know this sounds blunt but since this is a book dedicated to answering as many questions on the adoptive journey as possible, I have to be upfront. Foster-to-adopt is hard. It can nearly take the life out of you. While you'll have more money in your pockets (maybe), you will be drained. Out of the hundreds of foster-to-adopt families we know, none have had an easy journey.

That being said, there are a lot of beautiful moments along the way. Just this morning, as I was packing lunches for my children's school day, my teenaged daughter walked up behind me, out of the blue, and wrapped her arms around me, squeezing me tight. I jumped in surprise because this is not something she normally does. From her traumatic past, she tends to keep people at arm's length. She knows she does this…even admits it. We are used to her not showing much affection. It's sort of par for the course with this type of adoption. Not that this would not be the reality with domestic or international adoption, but it is very common with foster care and foster-to-adopt. Remember, you are caring for children who have gone through a significant amount of trauma. Some, you cannot even comprehend with your own mind because chances are you did not live through it.

Moments like the one I had this morning are rare but beautiful. Remember that if you choose this avenue for your adoption.

CHAPTER 6

The Art Of Fundraising

If you're anything like us, you stared at some of the numbers we just mentioned above with bewilderment and panic. Adoption is pricy. It can be overwhelming and all-consuming. It's suffocating to look at numbers ranging from $14,000-$50,000. In 2002 we had no idea how we were going to pay for our first adoption. We had some money in savings but Uncle Sam quickly showed up on our front door step to notify us that we owed him a whopping $7,000 on our Federal Taxes. We stood hand in hand, teary eyed and waved goodbye to our cash flow as Uncle Sam walked away with our money in hand.

When we asked our agency, they gave us the names and numbers of local banks who specialized in adoption loans. We started making calls. It will probably come as no surprise when I (Mike) tell you that most of the banks we talked to were welcoming us into their establishment with open arms. They were also welcoming us into unsecured debt. That was a fact we weren't clued into. We just thought that's what you do when you need a large sum of money. Now, 13 years later (and this might rub some of you the wrong way), we don't believe that's the best option. If you do want to learn about some alternatives to loans, keep reading....

A Better Way.

The phone call came on a typical afternoon. It was my friend John. We began with the typical salutations, inside jokes, and queries into one another's day. We had followed the same mode for thousands of previous conversations. As I spun in my comfy black office chair, John said something that was awesome and encouraging.

"Nicole and I have decided to adopt."
Awesome! I thought. "I'm excited for you bro!" were my exact words.

John and Nicole had practically walked side-by-side with us through our first few adoptions. They were more than friends. They were part of our family. They were the only people who visited us in the hospital when we adopted our first daughter. They watched our daughter while we took our foster care classes and stood beside us while we navigated the first rocky roads of adoption.

Needless to say, we were ecstatic for them. John continued, "And we've decided to raise the funds to adopt. We don't want to take out any loans!" *Wow,* I thought. *That's amazing, and wise.* As I listened to him the thought occurred to me- *I wish we would have done that for our first adoption.* Then, he asked me if I would join him in running a half-marathon to raise funds. I don't think I took one breath between his last syllable and my first. I remember thinking, *absolutely I will join you!*

I believed in this cause and I believed in adoption. In May, 2004, John and I ran the 500Festival Mini-Marathon in Indianapolis, IN to raise funds for their first adoption. "The Mini" as it's called, is the largest half-marathon in the United States. I won't tell you how we did because the paramedics advised us not to! (Kidding). In October of that same year, John and Nicole welcomed a beautiful baby girl into their family. It was an exciting journey and one we continue to share to this day, 10 years later. Needless to say, we are huge believers in adoption. But, we're even bigger believers in doing it debt-free.

John and Nicole discovered this firsthand. Once they shared their intentions to adopt, people from their church, their close friends and family, even co-workers began giving toward this cause. Folks fell in love with their passion. People who cannot adopt often love to get on-board with those who can.

You Can Do More When You're Debt Free.

You have so much more freedom when you're not chained to debt. And, just in case you weren't aware, children are expensive. You will pay a small fortune over the course of their lives and a lot of that expense is on the front end. Have you perused the baby isle at your local grocery store lately? That stuff is expensive. Like, *really* expensive! It's not getting any cheaper anytime soon.

Fundraising Ideas.

Because 12 years have passed and we've learned a lot, we've also discovered what we would have done if we could go back and do it over. We have listened to a lot of adoptive families share their hearts on this matter. Out of those conversations, we've come up with a list of adoption fundraising ideas.

These are not earth-shattering, mind-blowing, never-before-seen-or-heard-of ideas mind you! Here are several:

1- Host A Yard Or Garage Sale.

This is the most known and traditional way to raise funds. It may sound small but the return can be huge. I have seen people raise entire adoption fees ($15,000, $20,000 and more) through yard sales or garage sales. This option is also fun. There's a lot of community involved in yard or garage sales. If you can get your friends to participate it becomes a fun experience.

2- Run A Marathon Or Half-Marathon And Ask People to donate money on your behalf.

What makes something like running a marathon, or half-marathon, so great is that it puts a well-known activity or event on display along with your adoption. People can then clearly see that this is an actual event.

3- **Participate In A Walk-A-Thon**.

These are easy to organize and also a lot of fun, with that community aspect involved. You can host these easily by choosing a route around your town or your local mall. I have seen walk-a-thons raise as much as $35,000 in one day. The process is easy. Send out a notice to your friends, family, church members, neighbors and co-workers that you're holding a walk-a-thon to raise money for your adoption. It's even better, and more effective to find a campaign manager, or host, to talk and organize on your behalf. Once people sign up to walk, give them pledge sheets. Make sure there is a specific account set up for people to write their checks to. You can take donations for a couple of months before the actual event as well.

4- **Send Support Letters**.

If you've ever participated in a mission trip through a local church you're probably familiar with support letters and how they work. Formulate a letter to family and friends telling them of your opportunity to adopt. End your letter with a request for donations or prayer, or both.

5- **Google Search Grants**.

A simple Google search in your area will reveal tons of options. I live in Indianapolis and came up with over 500,000 results when I Googled "Adoption Grants in Indiana." You may also have success when you do a search of large corporations in your area. For instance, in Indianapolis we have the Eli Lilly Corporation, one of the largest suppliers of pharmaceuticals in the world. They have a huge heart for adoption and offer adoption grants to their employees as well as some community grants.

6- **Church Grants**.

If you are connected to a local church they may have grants available for pre-adoptive families. This is especially true if they already have an adoption or orphan care ministry. Check with your church but please do not join a church just to benefit from these funds.

7- **Sell Things You Don't Need Or Use Anymore**.

If you're anything like me you have clothes in your closet that you don't wear, tools in your shed you don't use anymore, or maybe even a third car you don't drive very much. As Dave Ramsey says, "Sell so much stuff the kids think they're next."

CHAPTER 7

If It's Meant To Be, It's Going To Happen

I (Mike) know you've probably had a million and fifty people say this cliche-ish sentence to you in your lifetime, but it's never more true than with the adoption journey. You may get matched with a birth parent through your agency, or a child in the country you're adopting from, things are looking up, you're getting excited, and suddenly the plans change. The birth mother suddenly changes her mind and the adoption is over, or the country closes adoptions from outside countries, and you've invested thousands into this process already.

These things happen all the time. We'll talk about how to navigate the emotions of a failed adoption a little later in this section, but I want to bring this up now because it's a reality. A lot of times we plan how the whole process is going to go, and we disconnect slightly from reality.

If it's meant to be, it will happen. I know this ticks you off. Heck, you probably have closed this book by now. If not, I am glad. I know this isn't easy to read, but you need to read it. And I need to be honest and say it (or write it). I say this because we needed someone to say this to us back in the day. We learned just how true it is that "if it's meant to be, it will happen." When our first daughter was born in 2002 we were at the hospital, the minute she was born. We had held her, watched her get her first bath, and I personally fed her for the first time with my own two hands.

A few hours later, we were told to go home. "The mother wants to keep her in her room for tonight," the nurse told us. *Wait...what?*

We drove home devastated. The case worker called us from our agency and said those words we hated to hear- "I know this is difficult but hang in there. If it's meant to be, it will happen."

Oh man, did they echo in my mind like someone yelling across the Grand Canyon! I hated every syllable of her words that night. But, she was right. Two days later we brought our baby girl home. It was a celebration.

Not so, 6 years later. Same agency, slightly different situation. A birth mother had chosen us and we were elated. What's more- she wanted to meet us for lunch with the case worker from the agency. "Are you kidding me?" we thought. We were even more excited. We jumped in the car on a winter afternoon and headed to a Max & Erma's restaurant on the Northside of Indianapolis. There was chemistry from the get go.

A week later, we paid $3500 toward the home study, birth mother living expenses, and a few other miscellaneous costs. For the next 2 months we stayed in continual contact with her. We encouraged her, prayed for her, and even talked on the phone with her several times.

But as her delivery date neared we began to hear less and less from her. She stopped taking our phone calls or responding to our emails. We heard those famous words again from the case worker- "Don't worry. Remember- if it's meant to be, it will happen." Oh, how we hated those words.

The week that she was to deliver, she changed her mind, notified the agency, and was never to be heard from again. That was devastating.

Here's the deal, though. A year later, we were chosen to adopt 3 little boys through our local foster care agency. We were overjoyed. That never would have happened if that adoption, a year earlier, had gone through as planned. The first adoption just wasn't meant to be. During that time of hurt we couldn't see the beautiful plan that had already begun unfolding.

Now, I have to be honest here. We are Christ-followers so we firmly believe that the Holy Spirit was in control and leading. Did we pray before the failed adoption? Absolutely. Since it failed, did it mean that God was not listening? Nope! Quite the opposite. He was listening and preparing our hearts for the joy of his unique plan.

If you're a praying person, let me encourage you before we move on. Prayer is so important to the adoption journey. Not just prayer, but faith as well. When we try to rush the process or control the process, we lack trust that our Heavenly Father is at work on our behalf and in our family's behalf!

CHAPTER 8

How Much Information Do You Share?

When we first adopted, we received some invaluable advice. We were showing our new daughter off, telling a little about the adoption journey, and trying to answer some rather blunt questions about our daughter's birth mom. That's when Dawn pulled us aside. Dawn was a member of the church we were serving with at the time, and, to this day, one of the sweetest, most genuine human beings we have ever had the pleasure of knowing.

"Your daughter's story is her story, and yours, no one else's," Dawn said humbly. "Be careful who you share her information with. You never want someone using your information against you or having someone repeat sensitive details back to your child when she is older!" She was right. We are eternally grateful for those words of advice. They shaped the future for us and still do to this day.

How do your share your family's story? It's tricky. Your family is obviously unique (whether it's built through adoption or the old-fashioned way). People will always be curious. But who do you share personal information with and how? The way we like to picture it is similar to how you would receive information about a novel. With every great novel you really get the details in one of three ways- *the back cover of the book, the cliff notes, and by reading the full-length novel itself.*

The "Back-Cover" Crowd.

These people are your passers-by. They're the waitress at your favorite restaurant. They're the nosey lady standing behind you in the grocery line check out studying your family. They're the folks who (bless their hearts) ask asinine questions like "are they real brothers and sisters?" They do not deserve an ounce of information but because you're courteous you give a nugget or two here and there. This crowd gets the general synopsis- "You adopted, your child has a special need, your family is different," but that's it. They receive enough to be intrigued but not enough to know specific details about you or your children.

They can judge or assume all they want, even ask specific questions, but you should never budge on your position with this crowd.

The "Cliff-Notes" Crowd.

This group receives more than the back-cover crowd, but not enough to formulate an entire book on your life. They know the details beyond general knowledge, and could explain your story to someone else if need be. They only know some of the intimate details of your children's story though. They are the friend from work, or the person in your church who takes a genuine interest in your family.

This group receives enough details to go beyond curiosity but not enough to enter into the inner-sanctum of your family. They would be further down the list of folks you would call in a crisis or when you needed to have coffee and vent.

The "Open-Book "Crowd

These people are your inner-sanctum, your support system, or your close friends. These are the folks who will walk through hell with you if you needed them to. They are steel traps, never sharing a drop of your information with anyone. They will sit and listen to you as you pour your heart out and not say a word unless asked. They do not give unsolicited advice and they never judge. This is the crowd who knows every intimate detail of your life and your children's. This group should always be kept very small.

Honesty Verses Privacy.

I'm sure you're wondering, after hearing about the advice our friend Dawn gave us, how you balance honesty and privacy. It's a big question. One we have had to wrestle with many times in the past. After all, you want to share your story of how you became a forever family because it inspires and encourages others who could eventually decide to adopt. But, you don't want to share information that could be used against your child.

I (Kristin) struggle with balancing honesty and privacy. As adoptive parents we respect the privacy of each child's personal story. It is their own to tell...or not. Our top priority is to protect. However our top priority as writers is to share. We have found strength in building relationships with others who have similar families. That bond is priceless. It is our desire to share some of our struggles with others so that they may find that strength.

It is also our desire to protect our children who have been through enough struggles to last a lifetime. We fear that as we share, we will open the door for prejudice and the judgment of our children and their birth families. This fear has been made real many times over the last 13 years. It has caused us to retreat and close our family off. We hope to find a balance that will allow us to share honestly about our struggles and successes in a way that will bring hope and healing to other parents.

Two of our children are diagnosed with Alcohol Related Nuero-developmental Disorder. Their brains were damaged by alcohol before they were even born. They struggle with anxiety, impulsivity, lack of focus, lower IQ, auditory processing, low tolerance for frustration, verbal communication and a rigid need for routine. They also have unbelievable creativity, strong imaginations, honest character, sensitivity to the emotions of others, generosity and compassion.

Many years ago, when both of these children were young, we joined a small group of friends that met throughout the year. Each time we had a get-together planned our sons would have a meltdown. Both children deal with a lot of anxiety around large groups of people. One son would refuse to get out of the car and the other would cling to me as if he was holding on for his life. After some time had gone by we told the adults in the group what we were dealing with. They were kind but immediately began to shake their heads in disgust at the choices of our children's birth mothers.

My husband and I began to back pedal but it was too late. Over the next few months we stood by and watched helplessly as our children were described as "a handful," or "difficult." I was dumbfounded as mothers of unruly biological children asked if I was ever able to find someone who could "handle" my sons so I could have a break? By sharing something that we thought would bring understanding, we had inadvertently handed others the freedom to criticize. We were sad and lonely. We did not attempt to share our story again for years.

When we joined an adoption class called Creating Attachment and Permanency at the Children's Bureau of Indianapolis we were skeptical. We sat rigid in our seats, mouths clamped shut during the first meeting. Then other parents started to share. Their emotions were raw. Their stories were sad, angry, frustrated, comical, hilarious and, most of all, hopeful. Our lips parted and the words came tumbling out. We finally knew there were other families like ours. We knew that it was time for us to face our fear, find a balance and share our story honestly.

Doing so has brought unbelievable freedom and healing to our family and our story!

CHAPTER 9

The Mental Shift

So there's all of the paperwork, the different types of adoption, the cost, the legal side, and the big questions when it comes to this journey. All important and all a major part of the preparation stage of adoption. There is also something that I (Mike) would call "the mental preparation" of adoption. One of the biggest things I hear post-adoptive families say is "We wish we would have been mentally ready. We were so exhausted from the whole process."

We understand. We wish we would have known the same thing. We walked into the first several months, even year, of our first adoption mentally spent. We felt like we had to play a mind catch-up for much of the first year or two. It was a big shift for us because that was our first child. For 2 and half years prior it was just the two of us. We stayed up as late as we wanted, slept in on the weekends, came and went as we pleased, ate whatever (and whenever) we wanted, and took road trips often. Now, we had a tiny human being to look after and keep alive. That tiny human being wanted to be fed every 2-3 hours all night long. She was one of those babies that woke up and went from 0-60 on the "feed-me-now" scale!

So what does it look like to be mentally prepared, or at least as close as possible to being prepared? There are a few things to keep at the forefront of your thinking that will help make that mental shift easier, and avoid as much exhaustion as possible.

It's a Journey.

One of the most important things you can do to make a healthy mental shift is plan for the long haul. Adoption could take months, even years. If you go into this process thinking that you will have a baby exactly when your agency estimates you will, you will be disappointed, and frustrated. If you have an idea in your head and you don't allow for any flexibility or alteration, you will find yourself spent and angry.

This is not an overnight process. This also is not like finding out you're pregnant and having 9 months to make plans. You could enter into adoption, be matched with a birth mother in another country, if you're adopting internationally, find out the baby is born, but not bring he or she home until they're 3 years old. In late 2004, we discovered pretty quickly, after one of our sons and one of our daughters came into our home through foster care, that we were going to adopt them. Their adoption wasn't final until the spring of 2008. Three and a half years later! That's a long time to wait. Even when working with a private agency, you may be told that you'll have a child placed in your home within 5 months, and after a year, you're still waiting. In our case, you could be planning to wait a year and bring your infant daughter home two weeks later. You may not have much time to prepare. Allow yourself to take a break. You won't always have everything in order, that's ok. Give yourself a chance to breath. Take this journey one day at a time.

It's Exciting!

This journey is unbelievably exciting. In fact, you probably experienced the excitement and joy just after you decided to adopt. You felt that rush of emotion. Your heart started beating fast and you realized that your life would never be the same. If you had children biologically, it was similar to the joy of finding out you were pregnant. This is excitement at work and it's a good thing. You should be excited about adoption. For all of the pain and agony that may or may not come from this journey, cherish the exciting part of it. Keep the excitement you have at the forefront of your thinking when the road becomes treacherous or dark. You may need to remind yourself, or have someone else remind you of the moments of excitement, when you're desperate and ready to quit!

It's Difficult.

We're no strangers to honesty. It's the overarching theme of our blog, confessionsofanadoptiveparent.com. We are not about to pull any punches here either. The adoption journey is difficult. Extremely difficult at times. It can leave you feeling broken, questioning and lost. This may be the most important mental shift you make on the entire journey. Plan for moments where you will feel defeated. Plan for exhaustion and frustration. You may feel this with the children you adopt, your biological children, or even your spouse at times. You may go through periods where you are mad at the world and you have no idea why. Your heart may break into so many pieces over the children you are caring for and loving that you aren't sure you can put it back together.

Adoption is also difficult because there are decisions to make, paperwork to fill out, high costs and the reality of loss. Somebody's going to lose something. Your child will have lost their birth parent, their native country, or their friends from the neighborhood they were removed from. You may lose the life you once fantasized about having, or quality time with your other kids. You may experience the loss of a child in the pre-adoptive phase. A birth mother may change her mind and decide to keep her baby. If you can make the mental shift into a realistic thought process, you will find strength for the journey.

CHAPTER 10

You Are a Part of Something Bigger Than Yourself

In 2008, just 4 years after we began taking placements through foster care, we had both *had enough*. One of the children in our care was diagnosed failure to thrive, requiring round the clock care, and multiple feedings daily through an NG-tube. If we pushed the formula through the tube too fast, she would vomit, and vomit a lot! To make matters worse, she was completely wild and out of control. At 2 years old she wouldn't make eye contact with us nor listen to anything we told her. Kristin and I looked at each other one night, around 2 or 3 AM, as we cleaned up the latest river of vomit, and knew exactly what the other was thinking- *"This isn't worth it!"*

One weekend became one month, one month became 4 months, and 4 months were quickly turning into an entire year. At first the birth parents were accusatory every time we had a visit with them. We couldn't do anything right. The case manager was cold and always preoccupied with other cases, and our other children were dealing with the trauma of watching their parents stretched so thin they could hardly make it to the next day. By November of that year, the children were reunited with their birth parents and we found time to breathe. Though that year was difficult, we were able to build a lasting relationship with the children's birth parents and extended family. We were able to advocate for them to get the resources they needed so that they could successfully raise their children at home. We realized that we were part of a story much bigger than ourselves.

Not What I Signed Up For.

A few weeks ago I listened to several men, all foster parents, pour their hearts out, and share their wounds. "This is not what I signed up for," one guy admitted, through tears. "I hate myself for some of the things that go through my head," another shared. "I feel like I'm failing." "I don't want to do this anymore. I keep asking myself when it will be over." Many of the children in their care were severely traumatized, difficult to handle, and out of control. It was taking a toll on them, their marriages and their biological or previously adopted children.

My heart broke for all of them because I shared many of the same wounds. I've walked the same road. I too have shaken my fist at the heavens and told God that, "This was not what I signed up for." I've looked at the children in our care and felt zero sympathy or affection toward them and hated myself for it. I have felt the frustration of trying to handle my out of control son while fighting off feeling like we'd made a mistake.

There were days, especially in 2008, where I would have quit foster care and decided no more adoptions on the spot if my wife had wanted to, no questions asked. But, as I stand here and look back on our journey, 7 years later, I am glad we didn't. We would have missed some amazing blessings that we couldn't see from where we currently were at that time.

You Have No Idea!

My 8-year old son Eli has an interesting perspective on the world around him. He makes me smile almost every day with the words he uses and the funny things he says. I look at his 2 younger brothers and feel the same way, Last night as I snuggled up to my 7 year old son, Jake, my heart filled up. "Gosh, I love this kid!" I thought to myself. "I couldn't imagine my life without him!"

If we had walked away from foster care and adoption in 2008 we never would have known them. The two of them, and our youngest son, Sam, came into our care in February 2009. When we were in the midst of our darkest moments in 2008 we couldn't see very far into the future. Nor could we have believed, for one second, that a day would come, years down the road, where things would not be as difficult or defeating as they were then.

You may not see the beauty of your story unfolding in the first 3 years, 5 years, or even 6. We didn't. We didn't see the beauty of our family really unfold until 2012, *ten years* after we first adopted. It was a hard, defeating, and exhausting journey. You may feel the same way right now. You may feel like this isn't worth it or that you made a mistake and you just want to opt-out! Hang in there. Stay the course. Keep moving forward. Don't quit! You have no idea what story your family will tell the world. It could be a story of hope, or one of overcoming all odds. You already are telling the story of redemption, but you may not see that story in it's full form, for years.

Its An Opportunity.

Many people get into adoption with this idea that they are a superhero on a rescue mission. That's not true. You adopt because it's an opportunity to change lives, not because you're amazing and you want to spread your awesomeness to others! You do it because you want to transform this world and bring hope where there is hopelessness. Remember that.

Right now there are between 143 million and 250 million orphans in our world. That's an astronomically high number of children without a home. That's an opportunity to make a difference. Currently, there are around 100,000 children waiting to be adopted in the U.S. That's an opportunity. These are children in need of hope, in need of a future, and they need something to believe in. That's an opportunity.

I am a firm believer that adoption has the power to change the world and shape, or re-shape, the future. I step into each new day knowing that it's an opportunity to make a difference in the world!

CHAPTER 11

Fear (The Great What If)

Let's talk about fear for a moment. Fear is real and fear will inevitably creep into your family in some fashion during your pre-adoptive journey. Fear has the power to insert itself into your life, and your journey. As Christ-followers we have a name for fear- it's Satan. He is our spiritual enemy. He loves to jump into your life, and into your head, and whisper lies to you. In fact, if he can't get you to stumble and fall in big ways with big glaring sins, he will try to make you doubt yourself, believe that you're failure, and want to give up.

Whether or not you have a faith-basis or a religious affiliation this doesn't change the fact that fear is a real and present force in your life and mine. We allow fear to dictate so much of what we do, and don't do. I (Mike) have done this quite often in my life. Sometimes a big decision is before me and instead of doing what I know I am supposed to do, or what I feel God leading me to do, I listen to the voice of fear. Fear comes in all different shapes, sizes, and voices...

"What if the birth mom changes her mind?"

"What if the country closes adoptions down?"

"What if the judge sends my child to live with an aunt in Virginia?" ·

"What if the birth parent isn't safe and puts our family in danger?"

"What if the child is sick and we don't have the means to care for them?"

"What if we can't come up with enough money?"

"What if we're missing something big?"

"What if we bring this child home and it doesn't turn out the way we hoped it would?"

"What if we're not supposed to do this?"

"What if I can't love my adopted child like I can my biological child?"

Fear throws a million "what-ifs" in your direction. Fear will always present itself at the most inopportune time. Fear has a way of getting into your mind and sabotaging your own voice, then using it against you. I'm not sure if you ever thought about the mechanics of fear like this or not, but that's exactly how fear stakes a claim in our lives. When you hear voices in your head saying, "You can't do this," or "This is going to fall through and you'll wind up without a child," it sounds familiar. That's because fear is speaking to you in your own voice. And normally, you believe your own voice. Fear never shows it's true colors, or uses it's true voice, because you would turn and run from it. The voice of fear disguises itself as the truth. Every time the excitement in you and your upcoming adoption grows, fear grows. Every time you celebrate a small victory, like completing your home study, being selected by a birth mother, raising some more funds, fear shows up. It's inevitable. In fact, even as I type these words, a small voice is whispering in the back of my mind- "no one cares what you have to say!"

Fear is no respecter of age, gender, socio-economic background, race, or creed. It strikes everyone at anytime. And with something as amazing, unique and life-changing as adoption, you can bet that fear will show up. In the 13 years we've been adoptive parents, we've heard fear speaking to us, but we've learned something very important about fear:

It lacks commitment.

Fear lacks commitment! The moment we decided to stop listening to that voice telling us to "go back, it's too risky, it's not going to work, this adoption isn't going to happen," it turned and ran. It didn't stick around. It stopped whispering to us. *Fear lacks commitment.* Call the voice you hear on the carpet and you can bet it will high-tail it out of there like it did for us. That's how you overcome fear. In fact, it's not that difficult. You just stop listening to it. You just keep moving forward. When fear begins to whisper, you work harder, move faster, run swifter toward your end goal of adopting a child.

The Other Voice.

Fear also works through other people. Particularly the people you are the closest to. Family. Close friends. Co-workers. Neighbors. People you know from church. Friends from a club or co-op. Fear isn't choosy. It uses anyone with a brain and a voice. It loves to sabotage the voices of those you are close to. But, this is *your* family we're talking about, not theirs. This is your future, not theirs. I'm willing to bet you didn't listen very much to those same voices when you bought your first house, or chose the car you now drive, or even decided to marry the person you married. Stop giving fear a foothold in your life through the words and actions of other people. Stand firm in your decisions and do not allow fear to use the voice of others to get you to second guess your adoption.

Turning The Tables On Fear.

It's high time you turn the tables on fear and stop allowing it to control you. Here's what I want you to do before you move on to Chapter 12. It's a short writing assignment. You can't claim that you're not a writer and therefore, opt out of this part. We'll know it if you do. (Just kidding). Take a sheet of notebook paper and write a letter to yourself from your soon-to-be-adopted child. Make it positive and encouraging. Leave any of your fears out of this. Write from the heart and mind of your future child. Ready? Set! Go:

Once you're done writing, lay the pen and paper down, walk away from it, and stay away from it for at least an hour. Go on a walk, exercise, take a warm bath, watch your favorite TV show, get coffee with a friend, etc. etc. See you in an hour!

Hours up. Now pick up the letter and read it. Soak in the positive words your child is saying to you. Consciously open your heart and mind to their words. Allow them to wash away your deepest fears.

Doesn't that feel good? Doesn't that make the fear leave?

Listen to me: you *can* do this! You are *called* to do this. This is *your* life, *your* family, *your* future!

Tell fear to take a hike!

CHAPTER 12

Debunking Big Myths

One thing that became quite evident to us, just a few short years after our first adoption was completed, was the misconceptions that the world around us had when it came to adoption. We talked briefly in Chapter 1 about how widely misunderstood adoption is. You will undoubtedly encounter lots of people, even your own family or close friends, who just can't figure out why you would do this. But you personally may have your own misunderstanding or misconception on adoption, or why you are doing this. I (Mike) understand this personally because that classified me before, and even after, we adopted. Not only did I misunderstand the whole process, but I also found myself believing in some big myths. It caused me to be very resistant, even in denial over what we were doing.

I'm willing to bet a few of you are in the same boat that I was. Maybe you are being controlled by things that just aren't true about adoption. Perhaps others have convinced you to be afraid of some things you really have no fear of or you've bought in to some of the worldly ideas about adoption. As you begin this journey, here are some of those big myths and what's really true about them:

Love.

Myth:

"I won't be able to love my adopted children as much as my biological children."

Truth:

Love is a choice, no matter what the situation is. You choose to love your wife, your husband, your children, your latte, your car, your dog, the list goes on. You choose to love the children God gives you, no matter their DNA. I feared this myth very briefly in the beginning of our adoption journey. But once my daughter stared into my eyes, and called me "daddy," the myth was dispelled!

Want.

Myth:

"I'm afraid my children will want their birth-parent(s) more than me."

Truth:

Your children will want their <u>mommy</u> or <u>daddy</u> and that's you! There will be days when they lash out, and scream "I want my 'real mommy,' or 'real daddy!'" It happened to us on quite a few occasions. And, yes, it hurt. It will hurt you too. But remember who picks them up when they're falling apart. Remember who kisses their wounds and wipes their tears away. Remember who is there to feed them and clothe them and listen to their broken hearts. It's *you!* They want *you.*

Confusion.

Myth:

"If I have an open-adoption with a birth-parent, my child will be confused."

Truth:

Your child will be confused over tons of stuff in life. This is a confusion that will not last. They will understand the difference between birth mom and mom just the way they understand the difference between grandmother and mother.

Truth.

Myth:

"It's better to wait until my child is older to tell them they are adopted."

Truth:

This is a huge MYTH! In our case, our first 3 children were African-American, so the joke would've been on us if we waited. Believing this myth does no good for you or your children. They will resent you. Be honest. Be open. And, by all means, celebrate their adoption. On a semi-related note- celebrate their birth parents too. Make sure you always hold your child's birth parent in high regard for making the choice to place them for adoption!

Judgment.

Myth:

"People will judge me and think I'm weird for adopting."

Truth:

This is actually true, but people are already judging you. There's nothing new here. You, and everyone else in this world, are being sized up, glared at, whispered about, gawked at, and pointed at all the time. Even if you can establish your life as "normal" in some way (not really sure what that means), you will still be judged for something. You can't escape it. I wrestled over being judged a lot, early in our adoption journey. When I finally realized that I couldn't escape it, I stopped caring about other people's opinions and focused on the most important thing- my beautiful family and my precious children!

Rescue.

Myth:

"I'm rescuing these children from a very bad place!"

Truth:

You don't adopt to rescue a child, you adopt to create a family and re-shape the future.

CHAPTER 13

Not Like The Movies

Our world, our culture, has a way of glamorizing adoption. We have the Angelina Jolie's or the Madonna's who jump on private jets to third world countries and "rescue" children. While there's nothing wrong with celebrities doing this, it's not representative of real-life circumstances. Ninety-nine percent of adoption cases are NOT going to unfold like this.

While we did bring some of our children out of difficult situations, we weren't rescuers, because adoption is not about going on a rescue mission. It's not about swooping into a war-torn zone and pulling a child out of certain death and despair. Adoption is about creating a new family, a new opportunity for the adult to be a parent and a new opportunity for the child to be raised by the parent. I (Mike) learned this back in 2009 when we were chosen out of 4 families to adopt 2 little boys, who were biological brothers. We looked at the pictures the case manager passed around and without even knowing them, or having met them, we just knew- "Those little boys are our sons!" It was meant to be. For the next 2 weeks we planned. We moved rooms in our home around to make space. We bought extra supplies (diapers, toys, clothes, etc.). We called our friends and family and shared the exciting news. We prayed. We anticipated. We hoped. And finally we went for our very first visit with them. But it did not go the way I expected it to.

They did not see us as the rescuers or even the parents. The older of the two just stared at us, saying nothing at all. The younger brother continually scooted away from us and cried, the entire time we were there. Finally, the older brother warmed up to my wife and actually let her hold him. The younger brother did as well, but hesitantly.

Once we got the boys home, a day later, we continued to see struggles. The older brother connected immediately but the younger did not. Our first trip to Florida with him was a disaster. He spent the entire week screaming, pulling my wife's hair, and throwing himself on the ground. As I watched this unfold, I found myself at a loss. This was not how I pictured this going, at all!

I, personally, pictured something like this:

We would rush to the foster home the boys were living in, scoop them both up, carry them to their brand new car seats, play Finding Nemo the entire ride home, and smile contently at one another as we listened to their sweet giggles from the back seat. In other words, I saw us rescuing them.

That was my first problem!

We weren't rescuers and this wasn't a rescue mission. We were adopting 2 little boys from a difficult place. My sons didn't need a rescuer, they needed a father. They needed a mother. They needed parents. And above all, they needed stability. In their short existence, they had traveled to several different homes and experienced a revolving door of people and faces. Some of their homes were with people who loved them very much but even that wasn't permanent. Nothing was forever in their little minds.

Here's what I've learned through my own personal growth experience in this area-

- **Open-mindedness not fantasy.** If your adoption experience is fueled by fantasy you are going to struggle more than you know. You need to be open-minded to the fact that your new son or daughter may be coming from

47

a difficult situation and that will prompt a lot of different emotions, behaviors, and reactions to you. Obviously this is slightly different if you're adopting a newborn baby, but if you're adopting from the foster care system, an older child domestically, or internationally, it's not a matter of "if," it's a matter of "when."

- **Unconditional love regardless of circumstances**. This is key because the circumstances could be very difficult or very hard to understand. Truthfully, we were blind-sided by this. We kept thinking that we were doing something wrong and that was why they were pushing us away or screaming in our face. However, the truth was that these behaviors were coming from a place of fear and the best thing we could do was love them deeply, no matter what we experienced!

- **A stable, consistent environment is key.** I can't say this enough! We're both huge fans of consistency. Nearly four years after bringing our sons home they are stable and grounded They are emotionally healthy and bonded. We've worked hard to make their lives consistent and stable.

CHAPTER 14

Dealing With Loss

Every good story has a conflict and a resolution. It wouldn't be interesting if there were no twists and turns along the way. The climax is in that moment where the reader just isn't sure things will actually end with happily ever after.

The Loss of "Normal"

When we adopted our first daughter I, (Kristin) felt a different type of loss. The first time I realized that adoption was going to be a different kind of parenting, I was talking with a group of young moms. I was holding my infant daughter in my arms when the conversation turned to breastfeeding. The moms in the group were criticizing women who chose to bottle feed. "I just love my baby too much to bottle feed." "It's an honor to know that I feed my baby with my own body." "It's so much healthier anyway." I wanted to disappear. I was overwhelmed with guilt that I could not provide for my daughter in the way that they could. I felt like there was a club for moms with bio children and I didn't belong. Before my children were adopted, I was not prepared for those feelings of inadequacy.

Empty Nursery

In the spring of 2004, we were all set to welcome a brand new baby girl into our home. We knew her birth mother had been told by her doctors of potential medical concerns with her unborn child. After some research we decided that if this were a biological child that we would accept whatever came our way. We proceed with excitement. Then came the call from a case worker. "She delivered, but the baby didn't make it." It was a crushing reality. A few days later we stood beside her birth parents at her grave, the weight of the loss, heavier than the earth above her coffin. The emptiness of the nursery pressed down on us as we arrived home after laying our little girl to rest. We had told no one, therefore we suffered the loss alone.

Another Empty Crib

As we shared in a previous chapter, in the spring of 2008, we had began the process of adoption again and had been matched with a spunky, upbeat, excited birth mother who was every bit as friendly. We took her to lunch, paid for living expenses, talked to almost daily on the phone, and then 11 days before she delivered, she dropped off the face of the earth, stopped taking our phone calls, stopped answering text messages. She was never heard from again. We disassembled the crib and packed up the baby clothes. We cried again, alone.

Dealing with Grief

Grief is not a weakness, it is a necessary part of healing.

In November, 2011, we lost a pregnancy. I (Kristin) was devastated. We had never had a biological child and had already been blessed with 8 children through adoption. God had given to us in abundance. I felt at first that my grief over the child would damage the emotional well being of my other children. I never wanted them to feel that I loved them less than the child that was biologically related to me. Like our previous losses, I stuffed the emotions till I thought I would burst. That's when I realized that my children were grieving along side of me. They had experienced a loss too. They were sad that they would not have a baby brother or sister. Once I realized their need to cry, I allowed myself to cry too. Admitting the loss was the first step in recovering.

Here are 4 key things you must do when you experience loss:

1- Grieve.

You've lost something. And that "something" was real. It was your child. It was your dream. It's okay to grieve. It's okay to feel the loss. It's okay to go through this for a while.

2- Wait.

Wait before you immediately jump into the adoption process. Give yourself some time to heal. The time you wait should be a time for processing, searching, healing, and restoration.

3- Lean.

Find someone you can lean on and spill your truck of emotions to. It needs to be someone who gets it and won't try to fix things right away with clever sayings or scripture passages. One of the healthiest things you can do through the adoption process is plug into a support system. These are people who know what you're going through as a pre-adoptive or adoptive parent.

4- Hope.

When the time is right, after you've grieved for a while or waited for some time, learn to hope again. Why? Because there *IS* hope.

CHAPTER 15

Adoption Language

One of the things you will learn, especially if you are just beginning the journey, is the vast difference between proper adoption language and improper adoption language.

If you find yourself cringing over some of the examples I use in this chapter, don't worry about it. I (Mike) remember sitting in that first adoptive parent meeting at Adoption Support Center feeling bad because I had just used some improper terminology with adoptive parents the week prior. I wanted to get up and call them right away to apologize. "Don't worry if you've said some of these things, or casually used some of these statements before," the meeting facilitator said. "You didn't know."

How To Respond.

I remember the first time someone used improper terminology in front of me. I was standing in our church lobby, holding my newborn daughter in my arms, and a well-intentioned elderly gentlemen asked if we were going to have any children of our own some day. I smiled and politely replied, "We're not sure what the future holds but we may have children biologically. We'll just have to see."

After stumbling over himself for a moment, and saying the typical, "Oh you know what I mean," he smiled, gave my daughter a grandfatherly pat on the head, and moved on. It's not that he meant to say the wrong thing, it's just the world he lived in had a limited understanding of adoption. The lingo matched the misunderstanding. Over the years, we've heard lots of incorrect terminology. Mostly, as in the case of the elderly man from our church, it's spoken with good intention. We know how frustrating this can be. Trust me, we've dealt with off-handed questions and comments toward us and our children more than we could count.

Here are 2 ways to respond:

Compassion: You were once in the dark too, so respond with the same compassion someone once responded to you with. View it as though you're bringing someone out of the dark and into the light.

Gentle Redirection. Simply respond with the correct terminology. There's no reason to be rude. You may be talking to future adoptive parents. Some people may be a little slower than others to respond. Firm redirection can expedite this. This may sound elementary (no pun intended), but make education your overarching goal. Adoptive parents, are interesting people. Our very presence begs others to ask questions. When we answer well, we are educating.

Improper Verses Proper

In our 13 years as adoptive parents, we've heard it all. Some of it has been quite offensive. So here's a run-down of incorrect questions and terminology followed by correct terminology, answers, and even some of the humorous answers we've been known to give. The goal of this is to help, not criticize! Please don't take it personally if you've ever asked one of these questions of an adoptive parent. We've all made mistakes.

- **"Do you have any kids of your own?"** or, **"Are any of your children natural?"** (trust me, this was asked of me recently). The correct way to say this is simply, "Do you have any biological children?" When we're feeling ornery, or just looking for a good laugh, we'll answer with something like,

53

"Oh yes, no preservatives or additives included! They're real flesh and blood human beings."

- **"Where did you get them from?"** or, **"Are they local?"** or, **"Are they from this country?"** The correct way to ask this is, "Did you adopt domestically or internationally?"

- **"Are they real brothers and sisters?"** When you adopt or foster sibling groups, you get this question all the time. It's understandable, but incorrect. The proper way to ask this is, "Are any of them biological siblings?" You could also ask, "Are there any sibling groups in your family?" We personally love to respond to this question with something along the lines of, "Considering that they fight all the freaking time, I'd say yes. They are real brothers and sisters!"

- **"Can't you have children?"** I'm just going to say it- pretty much NEVER ask this question of any adoptive parent, or human, ever, at any time. Adoptive parents, we recommend answering, "We chose adoption." It's a simple answer and that's the point. Of course, you could also say, "That's none of your business!" :-)

- **"Do you know their mom?"** This is a common question we've been asked. Mostly because several of our children were adopted through foster care. The correct way to ask this is, "Do you know their birth mother?" The way to answer is "Yes, we have a relationship with their birth mother," (If you do). To have some fun I like to answer, "Oh yes, I know their mother, I sleep with her every night!"

- **"Did their parents do drugs?"** or **"Was the mom homeless?"** or **"Was he a crack baby?"** These are examples of inappropriate questions that really shouldn't be answered, or addressed, but we will. In the past, I have kindly asked the person inquiring to step back and think about their question. Some questioning can be blamed on ignorance, and to that you simply shed light on their question. Other times, questions are just rude and off-base. Some of our children have come from difficult situations, but that's nobody's business but ours. If you're prone to ask questions, or be nosey, let me stop you. Asking questions like these are offensive and hurtful, especially if the child you're inquiring about is listening. For yourself and the adoptive parent's sake, think before you ask. If you are on the receiving end of this type of questioning, walk away.

Shedding Light, Asking Not

While some questions warrant an abrupt answer, compassion and redirection has made a world of difference. You may receive the rudest, most off-color question in the world. It may anger you so much that you want to scream. Do your best to respond with compassion. You will be glad you did.

If you're not an adoptive parent, or not educated on the adoption journey, or proper lingo, and you're reading this, here's some helpful advice- Think before you ask. An even better policy is "Ask Not." I know you're curious, and I know inquiring minds want to know. We've had so many people ask us about our story in the past. That's completely fine with us. We don't mind answering questions, but please don't pry. Don't snoop for info. This goes for all adoptive families. If we want to share additional information, we will. If not, we won't.

CHAPTER 16

Relating To Birth Parents

We love our birth families! They're an extension of our family. We can't express enough how important it is to have that perspective.

People will frequently want the skinny on your child's story. They may even feel entitled to the information. They may assume that your child's birth family is from a bad situation, a teenager, drug addict, in trouble with the law, or of a low IQ. One, or many, of these things may be true but a greater thing is true. They're the first parents of your child. They're the reason your child exists. They will pass on their own features. There's a strong possibility that your child will have his or her birth mom's eyes, nose, walk, or laugh. These things will be beautiful to you.

You will appreciate seeing your child's smile reflected on his birthmother's face because it's a smile you love and it's a gift she has given him. My rule of thumb with sharing our birth parent information is that if I (Kristin) would not share it about my brother or sister I will not share it about our birthparents. Your child may be very young right now or not even born but he or she will hear the words you speak about their family of origin. They will internalize those things and attach them to their own identity. God knew the exact two people that he needed to create your exact child. Your child may come from a less than desirable situation or even an unfathomably horrible one. This is information for you to know and keep private until the day arrives that your child is ready to talk about his or her beginning.

Our eight children are adopted from six different biological families. We have the honor and privilege of personally knowing all but one of those families. If you have the chance to get to know your child's birth family, we highly recommend it.

Fearing Birth Parents

We are frequently asked the question, "Aren't you worried they will come back and take her?" This birth mom has chosen me to raise her child. There is no greater act of trust and love that I (Kristin) can think of. This incredible woman placed her child in my arms and submitted to my authority as their parent. What an act of humility! I am honored to be entrusted with this great responsibility. I can't think of a person I would rather have in my court as I raise my child than the woman who gave birth to her, the birth father who gave her half her DNA, the grandmother that sat silently crying while she was placed in my arms.

I am not worried that my child's birth family will come back and take her. I am thankful for the love they've shown my daughter as they tried to choose the best life for her even when it wasn't with them. When I see them through the lens of the sacrifice they made, there is no fear.

Meeting For The First Time

We've had a lot of first time meetings over the years, and one in particular stands out in my mind. This meeting happened during the 9 years we were foster parents. One particular set of siblings had severe medical special needs. The parents were accused of neglect and so the children were placed in our home. We repeatedly took the children to their supervised visits only to return home and find out that the parents had reported us for one infraction or another- the baby's diaper was poopy, the 2 year old had a runny nose, the baby's tag was rubbing the skin on his back, just to name a few. Each visit was becoming more stressful than the last. One day as I drove to the visit I felt the knot tightening in my stomach. I asked God to help me see the birth parents through different eyes. When we checked in, I requested to talk to the birth mom and dad. I was granted permission, so as I walked the dingy hallway of the visitation center I began to see this situation from their perspective.

They had lost their children, they were accused of abuse and they were scared. By the time I turned the corner to see them face to face I had a heart of peace. I placed the baby in their arms, told them a funny story about the 2 year old and learned that the children's grandmother was in the hospital with maybe a few days to live. I knew I had to make a visit with her happen. Over the next 24 hours my husband and I were able to take the children to see their grandmother one last time. That act of compassion on our part changed the course of our relationship with the birth parents. The children did end up returning to their parents. We were able to attend doctor appointments with them, help find resources for the children and build a relationship that stands to this day. No matter what the circumstance, meeting a birth parent for the first time is scary. Put yourself in their shoes and try to see things from their perspective. Trust that God will give you the right words to say. You will be fine. Remember, they are probably more nervous than you are.

Writing Your Biography/"Dear Birth Parent" Letter

As Mike talked about in Chapter 3, if you are in the process of a private adoption, you will have to write a biography (bio) or "Dear Birthparent" letter. This is an advertisement for your family. Potentially hundred's of birthparents will read your write up as they choose the right family for their child. Remember that even though this may feel uncomfortable, this is a vital part of the process for a birthparent. They are able to get a snapshot of each of the waiting families. You want your family to stand out for the right reasons. It is important to highlight the things that set your family apart, i.e.- pets, vacations, family home, and hobbies. It is also important to show that you are real.

Before you begin to write, think of the things you would want in a family if you were the one choosing adoption. Write about those things. You will be surprised when you learn which part of your story stands out to the birthparent who chooses you. When our daughter's birthmother chose us she was drawn to the photos of our big front yard, our two dogs, and one of us sipping coffee. It turns out that when she was a child she always wanted a yard to play in and a dog to play with. She was also a lover of coffee. She felt like she liked us when she looked at the pictures. Don't try to be something you are not. Be yourself, let your personality and genuine emotion shine through your biography. You will be matched with the birthparent and child that you were meant to have as a part of your life.

When Birth Parents Can't (Or Won't) Have Contact

In our family, we see the value in having an open relationship with our children's birth families. We do our best to maintain contact with each of their birth parents. Sometimes that contact is not possible. One of our children has a closed adoption. Our daughter is constantly wondering about her birth-mom and her family of origin. This can be so frustrating for a child, however there are some things you can do to help your child feel some connection.

We help our daughter write letters to her birth family. She keeps the letters in a special place, some day she may have the chance to share them with someone in her birth family, but for now, they are her private thoughts. We also pray with her for her birth family and encourage her to talk about them often. When we see a good characteristic in our daughter we point it out and wonder aloud, "Do you think you get your elegance from your birth mom?" We point back to our daughter's birth family often but more frequently we point to the connections she has with the rest of her family and friends. Our daughter is a writer like us. She is also a singer like her daddy and an artist like her Grandma. She and her best friend enjoy acting in our local children's theater together. Our daughter also has relationships with many other children who are adopted. She has a safe place to belong among that group as well. She longs for connections from her past but she also lives in the connectedness of her every day reality.

When Birth Parents Are Not Safe

Do your best to live at peace with everyone. We have defused many potentially angry situations just by choosing to live at peace. We often set the tone for our interactions with birth parents just through our demeanor, facial expressions and tone of voice.

A few of our children have come from families who were no longer able to care for them because of dangerous or criminal behavior. They are currently, or have been, in prison. We have had to make some tough decisions about the safety of maintaining contact. We will do our best to address a few of the possible scenarios here.

Prison.

A few years ago we were court ordered to take our then, two-year old foster-son to visit his birth father in prison. We were worried about the lasting impact it might have on him. Years later, we realize we were right to worry.

Mike and I did our best to make the visit seem as natural as possible. It was difficult to calm our son's fears while ignoring the tightness in my own stomach. Our son seemed so small as I placed him on the floor to walk through the metal detector alone. He had been through so much that the very act of putting him down, was stressful for both of us. He clung to me as I talked softly to him. The guard was not the least bit patient so I pushed my son a little more quickly then normal. He timidly showed the bottoms of his feet and stood silently while the guard scanned him. My typically curious toddler waited with a disturbingly blank stare while my husband and I finished the initial safety checks. As each of the three steel doors latched shut behind us, I felt the grip of my little

60

one's hand tighten. He had no way of knowing this place was any different from the local shopping mall or office building, but he did. The silence of his typical chatter was nearly deafening. The visit itself was awkward but pleasant.

We exited just the way we came, carrying with us a quiet burden we hoped wouldn't weigh too heavily on the shoulders of our son. Many years have passed since that visit to the prison but our son still wakes with nightmares of being locked inside. At random times he'll phrase questions that begin with, "When I go to jail..."

You may not have a choice about visiting a birthparent in prison. If it is something you do need to do, my best advice is know that it will have an impact and be prepared for it. It may be very healing for your child to see the birthparent face to face. It may also stir up a lot of questions and fears that your child didn't know were lying under the surface. Always keep yourself open to talk with your child. Be aware that acting out behavior may follow a visit and reassure them that they are good, and safe and kind.

Abuse.

When children are removed from their first family because of abuse, it is likely that the family will not ever serve a consequence for their crime. If the child is in foster care, they will be required by a court to continue visits, often until the time of the finalized adoption. It takes a toll on you and your child. Monitor your child's behavior before and after visits. Document anything and everything. You may need to advocate for your child to get visits stopped. If you feel visits are harmful to your child, enlist the help of teachers, therapists, or court appointed advocates.

Emotional Abuse or Neglect.

When our daughter was younger, we had court ordered visits with her birth parents each week. We drove 30 minutes to a supervised visitation center each week. We arrived 15 minutes prior to the visit and waited with many other families in a dingy waiting room. Her birth parents were given until 30 minutes after the scheduled time to arrive. At this point, we were already an hour and 15 minutes into this commitment when we would be told, "Looks like they aren't going to show. You can go home now." I would strap the baby into the stroller and prop the three year-old onto my hip and begin the long walk down three flights of stairs. By the second flight my daughter would begin crying, by the third she was in a panic, "Where is my mom?" She would scream, "You won't let me see her, I hate you! I hate you." By the time we reached the lonely parking lot, she was a ball of snot and tears. In her fist, a fresh chunk of my hair. I would set her down inside the van, buckle the baby into his car seat and pull her onto my lap in the front seat. Pinning her arms to her side so she couldn't slap me, I would rock her and whisper. "I love you. I'm sorry they weren't here today. I love you." This continued for 4 years until her adoption at age 7. Eventually, the crying stopped, the disappointment stopped and the routine became a numb, soul heavy part of our week.

When the adoption was finalized, we had the opportunity to create our own set of rules. We were careful to sit down with our attorney and write up a plan that allowed for visits on our terms. We arranged for two visits a year, no drugs, no alcohol, and no no-shows. One slip up on any of these, and the deal was off.

In the years that have passed since those horrible visits, we've come to a place of mutual respect in our relationship. We've been able to meet at a park, pick birth mom up for church or even go out to dinner. What was once a damaging relationship is now a fun, healthy extension of our family. The key has been communication and clear boundaries. Our children are able to have relationships with their birthparents. The key is that they must be encouraging and safe. If at any point the children do not feel respected or safe, the visits are cut off.

When Birth Parents Become A Part Of Your Family

More often than not, we have formed lasting relationships with the birth parents and extended biological family of our children. Sometimes it's complicated to find enough chairs at the table for birthday parties but it's a problem we love to have! Each situation is different and each person in the life of your family should be treated as unique.

Often children who are placed for adoption still have loving biological families. One of my favorite stories is of the day we were chosen to adopt two of our sons. We went through an interview process with 3 other couples. We interviewed in front of a panel including the grandmothers of the boys. We liked them instantly and the feeling was mutual. When we were chosen to adopt the boys, we knew the grandparents would be a part of the picture as well. We were cautious as we got to know them but we were invited into a warm, welcoming family. They not only accepted us as the boys' parents, they accepted the rest of our children as well. Now, when Grandparents Day comes around at our elementary school, we have more than enough grandparents for our brood.

Hurting With Birth Parents

No matter the circumstances surrounding your adoption, your child and his or her birth parents have lost something. They lost their first family. When we put ourselves in the perspective of our child's birth family, we can see the loss and begin to grieve alongside of them. I was at the hospital with one of my children's birth mothers as she was told by child protective services that she would not be leaving with her newborn daughter. Logically, I knew she was at fault. She had broken the law and her choices put her daughter in danger.

She was also a mother just like me. I stood in the hallway of the maternity ward as the social worker exited her room. Her sobs turned to wails and her grief was palpable. I sunk to the floor outside of her door, my legs too weak to move. When I entered her room it was as a sister. A mother. I grieved with her. I shared in her pain. It opened my eyes to the pain each of my children's birth mothers must feel.

Celebrating With Birth Parents

We have had an opportunity to walk alongside the birth parents of our children in many circumstances. We have found that it is so important to celebrate with our children's birth families. Our children are watching to see how we respond to others. They delight in seeing us encourage and celebrate with their first family.

Healing With Birth Parents

No matter your circumstance, your child will need to heal from the loss of his or her first family. If you have access to your child's birth family this can be an easier process.

When my daughter was about 7 years old, her memory was triggered by a meal I was cooking. She came into the kitchen, stopped in her tracks and said, "My birth mom was making this meal when my birth dad hit her. She called the police and they put him in a police car. I watched him leave from the front door. He never came back." Just like that, a memory came back and she was able to articulate it. That night I called her birth mom and had one of the most difficult conversations I've ever initiated. I asked her if this memory was the truth, she said it was and asked if she could talk to our daughter and apologize. Healing began that day for all three of us. Not every birthparent will be willing to have these tough conversations but if both families are, the pay-off can be priceless.

Biological Siblings

As in any relationship, we believe it's important to treat each person as an individual. A relationship with your child's siblings might be abundantly beneficial or detrimental. Know the circumstances your child came from and view each situation from that perspective. Try to hear their words and actions surrounding conversations, or visits, with a birth sibling.

We have two extremes in our family. On one hand we have a child who is aware that she has birth siblings but has never met them. She takes great comfort in talking about them and dreaming about what they are like. On the other hand, we have a child who has a birth sibling living in our home, another who lives in the neighborhood behind ours, and another who visits often. She faces the unusual situation with an air of grace. She is sometimes embarrassed when people recognize that they all look alike but she usually just sees them as extended family. She views them more as cousins than biological siblings and in that way, we are all welcomed to consider her biological siblings as a part of our extended family as well.

CHAPTER 17

Healthy Attachment & Bonding

My Dear Friends,

We could write an entire book on healthy attachments and bonding. However, we just have time for one chapter. When a child first enters your home, they have suffered a loss. This was a difficult concept for me to grasp when we brought our first daughter home. I (Kristin) didn't want to admit that she had lost her first mom. What I did understand though was that I had missed the first 9 months of her life. Inherently, I knew that I needed to cherish each moment from that day forward. I subscribed to baby wearing and co-sleeping for the first year of her life. When others would criticize me for carrying her as a toddler, I diligently ignored their comments. I knew there was a difference between bonding and spoiling. What I was doing was bonding.

We're 13 years down the road from that first experience. Here are a few things we've learned:

Patience

Bonding will take time. I remember longing for a real hug from my daughter. I waited almost a decade. My daughter came to live with us when she was 3 years old. She had witnessed domestic violence and was the recipient of emotional abuse and neglect. For years she would allow us the occasional stiff hug but nothing more. We never snuggled during our bedtime routine or held hands in public. When she scrapped her knee she would accept a bandage but refuse any physical comfort. We continued to wait patiently. Shortly after her thirteenth birthday, I was carrying a load of laundry up the basement stairs and chatting with my daughter about her day at school. Without any warning, she put her arms around my waist and squeezed, "I love you Mom." I froze, put the laundry basket down and enjoyed the brief moment. That genuine, real hug I'd been longing for was worth the wait. Be patient with your little ones. They are learning.

Pursue

When my daughter was a teenager, she lost her birth father. His death was a tragic surprise and no one knew how to deal with it. After years of loss and uncertainty, our daughter had learned to stuff her emotions inside. We took her to counseling but it was an uncomfortable dead end of coloring pictures and silly projects. When she wanted to quit, we let her. Occasionally, I would take her to coffee, or a day of shopping to try to talk about her feelings. She politely refused to answer truthfully, "I'm fine. Everything's ok." I felt helpless and as time went by, I stopped asking. Now that my daughter is an adult, she struggles with anxiety an unmanaged grief. I wish desperately that I could go back and pursue her more diligently. I could have searched for a more well-equipped counselor. My advice to anyone who hopes to build a bond is to pursue. Our children are often missing the skills to develop and maintain healthy relationships. It 's up to us to show them how. We have to pursue them.

Consistency

Consistency is key! When our son came home, he was 11 months old. He had lived in a total of 5 homes and was distraught to say the least. From the moment I picked him up at his foster mom's house, he clung to me for dear life. Literally, clung. He clawed at my face, grabbed handfuls of hair and screamed in terror if I put him down. So I didn't. I held him for a year. He attended church with me, slept in my room, sat on my lap and held my hand while I drove the car. A little at a time, he relaxed. He sat on his dad's lap. Held his grandma's hand. Let his auntie carry him on a family hike. For a short time, I left him with a sitter. I asked his sister to bring him a sippy cup of milk.

I noticed he began to play a little farther away from me each day, glancing to see if I was still watching. Though frustrated, our family worked together as a team to slowly gain his trust and teach him to trust the world around him. Children who have experienced loss and trauma in their early years of life, have lost the opportunity to learn the very basics of human relationship and trust that is learned in infancy. With consistency, a child can re-learn the parent/child relationship. As I watched my son trot off to the bus this morning without even a glance back, I can barely believe that this is the same child from 6 years earlier. Consistency pays off.

CHAPTER 18

Trauma

A Realization and an Understanding

I (Mike) knew something was wrong when our son wouldn't stop crying. I had only been a parent a few short years, and he had only lived with us for a few months, but in my gut, I knew. It was a warm, sunny, fall day as we trotted across a college campus behind a group of high school seniors we had volunteered to bring for a college visit. With every step our son cried louder, and longer. The tour guide glanced annoyingly at us several times throughout, and the students were trying to ignore his screams.

It wasn't just screams or cries; it was aggression. He clawed at my wife's face. A few times he even tried to climb up her sweater and over her head. I lagged behind, annoyed and frustrated. "Why wouldn't he just shut up?" I thought to myself. "This is embarrassing and there's no reason at all he should be crying like this! I wish he would take his hands off her face." It was easy for me to believe this. It was even easy for me to say this. But what I didn't know was that his behavior wasn't an act of defiance (after all, he was only a year old). It wasn't even on purpose. The tears, the screams, the clawing, and the outbursts were all a result of trauma.

You see, before my son was born, he'd been exposed to drugs and alcohol. After his birth, he bounced from apartment to apartment and eventually into a homeless shelter. He was malnourished and exposed to domestic violence. We couldn't begin to imagine what this was like. We couldn't even identify or understand. The trauma his little mind had been exposed to was more than any one human being should face or ever have to deal with. When my son was much older, his inability to manage his former trauma became exponentially greater. So did our misunderstanding and our own secondary trauma.

This past December we were in an all-out battle with our son. He was completely out of control, screaming, spitting, cussing and cowering next to the claw-foot bathtub in our upstairs bathroom. He then tried to push the tub off over with his head. Tears soaked his cheeks, and snot ran from both nostrils over his upper lip. He was out of control and violent. We were at a loss. In fact, we were angry. Our other children were downstairs with their older sisters, nestled on the sofa, for family movie night. We were dealing with this!

My human-instinct wanted to throw him out of the house, into the cold, and leave him there, just to show him that this kind of behavior was absolutely unacceptable and that our other children did not deserve to be treated this way. I also wanted to show him who the boss of this house was. He was not in control. He was not going to dictate, any longer, the course of our day. We were exhausted. Meltdowns like this had become a daily ordeal. Something didn't go his way- tantrum! He didn't get the answer he wanted- violence! We had other things on the schedule and he had a shorter amount of time to ride his bike outside- outburst! Meltdown after meltdown; sometimes for hours.

As I stood in the bathroom staring at him in a ball on the floor, moaning like an injured animal, I fumed. *I'm missing time with my other children because of this crap*, I thought. But then, through the tangled mess of my frustration, a thought pierced my mind- "He's afraid." I tried to ignore it. I even tried to refocus my thought process so I could retain my anger. My attempts were futile. Slowly, as if floodwaters rose to overtake a shoreline, my anger was overtaken by compassion.

Standing in our bathroom, on that winter evening, I saw my son in a new light. I shut the bathroom door, moved closer to my son, knelt down, gently placed my hand on his shoulder and said, in a whisper, "I know you're afraid buddy. I know you don't want to hurt any of us or ruin this night. I know there's something deep inside of you causing you to act this way and it's not your fault."

It's not your fault.

Here's a valuable truth that you need to hang on to if you're going to successfully travel down the adoption road: the likelihood of adopting a child who has gone through some form of trauma is great. If you foster-to-adopt it's even greater. Children adopted internationally may have faced the trauma of living in an orphanage, being on the streets, malnourished or abused at the hands of older children. Within the the foster care system children may be exposed to drug abuse, domestic violence, sexual and physical abuse, movement from foster home to foster home, and the trauma of birth parents not showing up to visitations. I can't begin to imagine what it's like to walk a mile in their shoes. Even as I type this, I'm thinking about the toughest, most traumatic ordeal I went through as a child. It doesn't compare.

When you have a child who was exposed to drugs or alcohol while in the womb, or physical abuse while in the womb, there is a part of their brain that is damaged. It's the heartbreaking and devastating truth of trauma. We are raising several children who suffered brain damage due to a choice their birth mother made. I have had many moments in the past where I felt physical anger toward my child's birth mother for the choice she made to drink while he was in her womb. I've personally grieved the decision she made to put her cocaine addiction above the health of her unborn child. I find myself unable to escape the frustration at times. When I look at my sons, or my daughters, I see amazing, beautiful, talented, funny and gifted children. For their entire lives they will live with a part of their brains missing. That's infuriating! It's ok to be mad about it, but the anger gets us nowhere. We can't do anything to change what has happened to our children, what we can do is love our children for who they are, completely and wholly.

A Place Of Fear

That night I realized my son was afraid, he was speaking from a place of fear and I didn't even realize it. I couldn't hear it because I grew up in a typical household, with typical parents, who never laid a hand on me (unless I needed my hind-end tanned for misbehavior). I was never starving, nor was I afraid someone would charge into my bedroom, yank me out of my bed, and beat me. I never feared loosing our house or that I would end up in a shelter somewhere. I never watched my mom take a beating from her drug dealer. I couldn't imagine ever seeing this, even as an adult.

If you're the parent of a traumatized child you know this place. These are the dark places our children speak from. The behavior that drives us nuts or terrifies us is an outcry from a desperate place we know little, to nothing, about. For our children, that place of fear is real.

A Place Of Abuse

My mom never used cocaine or marijuana when she was pregnant with me. She took care of herself. When I was a child my dad never slapped me or punched me in the back of the head for walking too slowly. I never watched my dad beat up my mom either. My son experienced a lot of this as an infant. Several environments he was exposed to, before he came to live with us, were volatile and dangerous. He experienced abuse and he witnessed abuse. To this day, anytime we drive through urban areas in our city, he is uneasy. They resemble a fuzzy memory of his past and bring back visions, images, and memories he's tried to bury deep and forget about.

A Place Of Uncertainty

When I was in 6th grade my parents signed me up for a week of summer camp. I had never been away from home for more than

1 night, but this was going to be 6 whole nights! Midway through the week I lost it. I wanted to go home so badly that I nearly lost all ability to function. Finally, I got ahold of a telephone and called my dad. He came within the hour and picked me up. The freedom I felt that evening, as I walked through the warm grass of our backyard, was overwhelming. I choked back tears the entire time. I was so relieved to be home.

Home. It's what brings us ultimate security as children. It's what gives us confidence to face each day. It's what makes us feel safe and secure, knowing that our mom or dad are there and will make sure we are taken care of. For a child who's been removed and placed in foster care, confidence and security blow away like a leaf in the wind. The uncertainty of being removed from one house, placed in another, and then another, and then another, cause a child to look at the world with deep uncertainty. These are wounds they carry with them for a long time. These wounds cry out through outbursts, fits of rage, lack of respect, and lack of attachment.

Why? Because when a child believes something's not long for this world, he instinctively detaches himself from it. His behavior changes to accommodate the change in scenery. In his mind, he tells himself, "If I'm going to move to a new home anyway, why get attached? Why form a bond? Why listen to a word these people say?" There's a disbelief that any home will be a forever place.

Love Through Fear

We don't tolerate our son's out-of-control behavior. In fact, he doesn't live with us right now because of this. He is attending a boarding school for now. One thing we have learned to do is love him through his fear. It's not easy. It's extremely difficult and unbelievably exhausting. The hardest thing you may have to do is stay consistent and firm even when your child is pushing every single button and challenging every single boundary you have. We've been through this and have the battle scars to prove it. That night, in our bathroom, I ended up sitting on the side of the bathtub, for an hour, holding my son close. He tried to push me away but I stayed until the walls came down. It wasn't easy, but it was a sacrifice I needed to make. I realized that night, that I needed to stop fighting against him, and start fighting for him.

We know how hard it is to parent a child from a traumatic past. We have navigated attachment issues, violent outbursts, and exhausting meltdowns, time and time again. Choosing love is the hardest thing to do in those moments. Choosing to fight for your child may take the life out of you. Have hope, it is worth it! You have the child you were meant to raise. You were meant to be their mommy or daddy. Somewhere, somehow, their life will change, and so will the future, because you chose to stay, you chose to fight....you chose to love!

Understanding Fetal Alcohol Spectrum Disorder (FASD).

We've included a section in this chapter on FASD because of the overwhelming number of children born with it every year, and the commonality of it in either international or domestic adoption cases. In fact, the statistics are staggering. It is estimated that 40,000 infants are born with FASD every year (Source- nofas.org). Two to five percent of all babies born in the US ever year have been affected by their mother's consuming alcohol during their pregnancy.

While these numbers are shocking and angering, there are doctors today who still tell expecting mothers that alcohol in moderation during pregnancy is okay. However, there is no good evidence on a safe amount of alcohol during pregnancy. There simply isn't a "safe amount."

For the majority of the world, Fetal Alcohol Spectrum Disorder (FASD) is misunderstood and often judged. But, there are powerful truths that can change your life when you understand, and embrace them.

Anger.

That's the word that comes to mind when I think about FASD. Anger.

I'm angry that my child's birth mother would make the selfish choice to drink during her pregnancy, angry that the claws of addiction dug deeper than the conviction of pre-natal care, angry at the numerous therapists, doctors, and authorities who've downplayed or disagreed with my child's diagnosis over the years, angry at a world that judges before seeking the truth, and angry when I think about the missing pieces of my child's life.

The child I chose with love.

Most of all, I'm angry that he will never have a normal childhood. A part of his brain is absent thanks to a stupid choice, a lack of self-control, and an unwillingness to guard his precious life before he took one peek at the world. I know this sounds harsh but this is the stuff I wrestle with often. Sometimes it eats at me, grinding away at my soul like a jackhammer grinding away at concrete. Other times, it's sadness. A deep longing to go back in time, before his conception, and beg his birth mother to not make the choice she would eventually make.

Yes, we reel in pain over this disease. After all, that's what it is. It's brain damage, and the worst kind too, as far as we're concerned. We live with the devastation of our child's violent outbursts that have brought trauma on our family so deep that we're not sure we'll ever heal from it. We wrestle but, we're hopeful. In the midst of our life, which often looks more like a pile of ashes than a life, we have a hope and a belief that our child, our son, will succeed. It began a while ago, when we embraced some powerful truths about FASD...

1. **It's a permanent condition**. FASD is permanent brain damage. It cannot be reversed nor cured. The part of the brain that is affected will never heal or be restored. When

we finally stopped fighting against this reality, and stopped trying to fix our son's physical condition, we discovered something revolutionary (more on that in a minute).

2. **It's an uphill climb**. Everyday of our child's life will be an uphill climb, and it will be so for you if you have a child who suffers from this. You'll fight with them, and against them. Heck, you'll spend a ton of time fighting professionals who just don't get this disorder. You will feel like you're climbing the side of a mountain but never reach the summit. Honestly, it's painful, and exhausting. Doesn't feel very hopeful, right?

3. **No amount of alcohol is okay**. There is no safe amount. One drop at any given moment during pregnancy can cause permanent damage. We are astounded that doctors still tell women today that they can have a glass of wine or a small drink every now and then while they're pregnant. In our opinion these doctors should be barred from practicing medicine for eternity.

4. **It's misunderstood**. Recently, Kristin was watching YouTube videos on the NoFAS website when one woman stated, "FASD doesn't get the attention it deserves because it's not a 'designer' disorder like autism." True! There is a vast misunderstanding surrounding FASD.

5. **It's often judged**. Even though it's clear that we are adoptive parents (our oldest son is African-American), we have been judged. My wife, mostly, as a mother, has faced judgement even though she is not his biological mother. This stems from the misunderstanding we just talked about. It's also inaccurate education on the realities of FASD. But....

6. **It's not the end**. Reading those first 5 truths feels depressing and dark. I know. I wrestle with them all the time. Every time I look at my children who are affected by FASD I feel a mixture of anger and sadness. But I've discovered there's hope. This is not the end, even though it feels like it when you're crawling through the trench. This is not a wrap on our child's life. And, here's why...

7. **It's a fight**. You and I are locked in hand-to-hand combat as parents. Yes, with our sons and daughters because, let's be honest, the days of parenting a child suffering from FASD are dark and un-ending. But this fight is much bigger than anything we've seen. It's not a fight against our children, it's a fight for our children. It's a fight for their heart because we love them. I love my son more than anything and that's why I'm choosing to fight for him, even though I sustain deep wounds! I will not stop chasing down resources or finding outlets who get this disorder.

8. **It's not a life sentence for you -or- your child**. While this disorder is permanent, this is not a life sentence unless you let it become so. It's your choice. The world is slowly starting to wake up to the reality of FASD and great resources are starting to take shape. NoFAS.org is one of those. This website is packed full of insightful and inspiring content, plus resources that can help navigate the trials of parenting a child with this disorder. One other resource that we are huge fans of is the documentary Moment to Moment which can be found by visiting www.NTIUpstream.com.

9. **It can't be cured but it can be flipped on it's end**. It's all comes down to whether or not you choose to keep fighting for your child. The world may see my children as hopeless or damaged, but I see my child as a promising human being filled with talent, creativity and the ability to overcome this and succeed.

10. **The disorder can't be changed, but the heart can be**. We are committed to helping my son's heart heal. In fact, it's our daily prayer for him. We believe this is the answer for FASD. He will always wrestle with the side-effects of this disease. He will always deal with impulsivity and a thought-process that fails him, but, the healing of his heart is how he will beat the odds and overcome this. Nothing in this world can make us give up on him, or this truth.

As I write these words, my oldest son, who has been in and out of residential facilities for the past 5 years, thanks in part to his violent behavior, brought on by FASD, is moving to a new facility even farther from our home. Many would read those words and immediately place blame on us. Frankly, Kristin and I have wrestled with that already. We've laid awake many nights, over the past 5 years, asking God what we did wrong, begging Him for an answer. We've watched the way other children (and adults) have treated our son, judged him, and his disorder. We've stood helpless as our son caused a scene in public or flew into a rage and hurt one of our other children or us.

Yet, we won't give up. As we grapple with the truths above, we find power through them. We find the will to fight. As the reality of his condition and the condition of hundreds of thousands of other children like him, sink in, we find ourselves invigorated and motivated. The hope that we have is the hope we choose to seize. We could give up and allow our son to remain a statistic, or we could keep getting up, even when we're knocked down hard, and help our son become a success! We choose the latter.

CHAPTER 19

When Other Parents Don't Understand

Honestly Speaking

My son's coach meant well. He really did. His fatherly instincts told him to comfort my son and try to remedy the situation by loaning him his gloves. The temperatures at game time were a brisk 30 degrees. The sun was up, but slow to melt the frost that fell in the early morning hours when it was the coldest. My son stood on the sideline shivering, crying, snot running down his upper lip, and looking as if he were close to death.

I (Mike) stood on the opposite sideline, glaring at him and feeling no sympathy as he played up his sob story. I fumed as I reflected back on the night before, when I was digging out knit caps and gloves in preparation for his game. Because I'm a college-educated person I paid attention to the evening weather report (which a kindergartener could do). I listened when the reporter said, matter-of-factly, that the next morning temperatures would be below normal. He even went as far as to say, "If your son or daughter is playing soccer, football or fall baseball, you will want to dress them warm for morning games!" Imagine that!

My son argued with me. He told me that he didn't need to wear gloves, because none of the other kids would be. He shook his head and told me that football players are supposed to be tough and wearing a knit cap would make him look like a sissy. He then obsessively walked around the house in his uniform pretending to be an NFL player who didn't wear long sleeves in frigid temperatures. Big talk until he got out of the car the next morning and joined his teammates (who, by the way, were all wearing knit caps and gloves). He almost immediately started to shiver. I didn't budge. "Life lesson learned," I thought to myself. "He can freeze his 'you-know-what' off!"

Some of the parents nearby gave me nasty looks. Some tried to remedy the situation by getting involved. I'm sure I was pegged as a terrible father. But the highlight of this whole experience had to be the email I received from his coach, later that afternoon, saying "Next time we have a game with those temperatures please make sure to properly dress your son." He then explained his strategy for making sure his son was dressed for chilly game-time temperatures.

And that's when it hit me- This world will never understand how or why I parent my special-needs son the way I do, and that's okay! Many would look at that experience and chalk it up to normal 9-year old behavior. But that's not what it was. What people rarely see (unless they spend significant time with us) is the impulsive, illogical, obsessive behavior my child displays over nearly everything. He has a disconnect in his brain. It's a permanent condition he inherited from the choice his birth mother made to consume drugs and alcohol when he was still in her womb. While other children may argue with their parents, push buttons, stomp their feet and demand their own way, my son obsessively makes it a campaign, battles us to sometimes violent levels, and refuses to listen to logic, even when logic is causing his ears and finger tips to turn blue and go numb.

It's a common thing that adoptive and foster parents deal with- the misunderstanding of most of the world around them. It comes in many forms- glares, nasty comments, even judgment. This is the unique world of raising a child that we didn't biologically create, and certainly didn't cause the trauma that they deal with every day of their lives.

If we could say a few things to parents who have not adopted, or are not raising a child with attachment disorders, ARND, or severe trauma from their past, it would be this:

"I'm blunt and to the point for a reason."

When you live with a child who has brain damage and a mental illness, you can't leave an ounce of what you say up for interpretation. My son will fill in the blanks and many times that equals disaster or a very bad choice. I have to be blunt and to the point, always. It sounds harsh at times. I know this. My point must be crystal clear with my child. I stick to a strict schedule with him. Bedtime is always the same. So are trivial things like brushing teeth, household chores, and homework. Without a routine, my son will melt down.

Most parents only have to give gentle reminders to their child (usually). And even if they goof and forget, their parent can remind them and they'll do what is asked of them (most of the time). Not so with a child who has come from a traumatic past or suffers from something like Alcohol-Related-Nuerodevelopmental-Disorder (ARND), or reactive attachment disorder. If I gently remind my son, he won't get it, or he'll snap and throw a 2-hour plus tantrum. If I resort to doing the task myself he'll never learn nor come back to the task in his mind. I have to bluntly state my expectations and be ready with a consequence if he fails to do what was asked of him.

"I give the consequences I give for a reason."

In his mind, he believes he is right and I am wrong, all the time. Not only that, he has learned the art of trickery and manipulation. This is a derivative of reactive attachment disorder. If he can get you to buy into his story, believe that I just didn't want to give him gloves and hat for the freezing temperatures, he wins, and quite frankly, you lose. He doesn't necessarily mean to do this but his brain has been damaged. He isn't thinking logically and, although I reassure him and show him that moms and dads always take care of their children and are there for them, he reaches for something else. Many times, it's a stranger or a person (like a coach or teacher) that he barely knows.

I give the consequences I give because the only way he'll learn how to live is through the structure I keep in place. Because his brain is damaged there is deep seeded fear and anxiety in him. That manifests itself in impulsive choices, and sometimes, obsessive, violent outbursts.

"You have no idea how exhausting this is."

You who parent typical children, with "normal" brains, who pull normal child-like stunts, fail to understand that I have to be vigilant around the clock. I cannot take my foot off the gas. I have to read labels for ingredients you never give a second thought to. I have to ask questions at doctor's appointments that most parents never have to ask. I have to mentally and physically prepare for something as simple as a trip to the grocery store. I have to make sure my son is following the same routine, day after day after day.

While your child can get off schedule during vacation or a weekend, mine cannot. The consequences of this could take days or weeks to undo. I don't expect you to understand the way I parent my special-needs son, but I am asking for respect and a little less judgment. Until you walk in the shoes of a parent with a child who has special needs you will never understand the reasons why we parent the way we do.

In case you're wondering, I secretly brought his knit cap and gloves to the game that day. After allowing him to live with his consequence for a while, and refusing to let his coach bail him out, I walked over, reminded him that I was his parent, and gave him his cap and gloves.

CHAPTER 20

Telling Your Child's Story

No matter the age of our children when they were adopted, we love to tell the story. Some of our children have stories that are filled with grief, loss, abandonment and terror. All of our children have suffered at least one loss, the loss of their first family. When we talk privately with our children we address these issues with compassion and patience. When we talk around the dinner table, or while playing outside, taking a walk, or sharing a cup of coffee, we tell a different story. We tell our children about the joy of seeing them for the first time. We tell how we feel about being their forever mom and dad.

We tell about times that our child made us laugh or times that our child made us proud. Like every family, we have that one funny story about tripping over nothing. We have the ever-standing battle about who makes the best biscuits and gravy. We love to tell the "remember when" stories. Our children's stories are often sad, but that isn't all they are. Find the joyful part of the story and tell it over and over. Fill your child's heart with the knowledge of joy that being a part of their story brings.

Telling Their Story

A dear friend of ours shared this bit of advice when our first daughter was born. She explained that even though we were excited and wanted to shout our daughter's story from the roof-top, we should take caution with the information we shared. She explained that some people will treat her story with the respect that it deserves, but others will not. There is always the possibility that someone may use our daughter's story as a weapon. It is her private information for us to keep safe for her. One of our jobs, as we prepared to bring her home, was to guard her story. As she has grown older she's inquired about her birth parents and relatives. We talk with her about the information, as it is age appropriate. We've extended this caution to her as well.

She may choose to share her story with friends and family but she may also choose not to. It is entirely her information. We are so thankful that we heeded the advice of our friend with all of our children. Six of our children are adopted from foster care. The principle of privacy has served us well especially in those adoptions. Some of our children have painful histories. Our commitment to protect the intimate details of their life has allowed our children to heal in their own time and maintain their own distinct sense of self as they find their place in the uniqueness of having two families.

Helping Your Child Tell Their Story

In our local elementary school, each family with a student in second grade has the opportunity to be a surprise reader in the classroom. As luck would have it, this has always been the same year that peers started noticing that our children had a different type of family. With our child's permission, we used this "special reader" project to write a book of our own, explaining the journey of adoption. We add a small section at the end for appropriate adoption language. We have written and illustrated a unique book for each of our children. We used age appropriate phrases like, "Mike and Kristin loved their family very much but felt that something was missing. When they got the call from the adoption agency, they were very excited."

We read these books to the class and gave our children a chance to talk to the class too if they wanted. (They've always let us do the talking and that's ok too!) It's very important to be truthful with your child about his or her story. We are very careful to give our children positive phrases about adoption and an "out" or a phrase to use when someone is being too nosey or rude. Your child may want to share his or her story and that is great. When our child does not want to share, it's vital that we prepare them to set boundaries. It's absolutely acceptable to teach them to say, "I don't want to talk about that. That is my private story." Or, "I'm not comfortable sharing that with you." It is our job to empower our children to take ownership of their own story.

When Strangers Get Nosey

We've all had it happen! The lady behind us in the grocery line just keeps asking questions. Remember, your story is your story. Do not ever feel that you have to answer anyone's question. It's good to be kind but it is not necessary to cover for someone's ignorance. Educate when you can but if a person is downright rude, walk away. Your children are watching and listening to everything. Make sure they see you unshaken by the ignorance or stupidity of others. You owe the stranger nothing.

CHAPTER 21

Unexpected Blessings

Adoption is worth it. You have no idea what story your family will tell the world. Our family has been through the ringer. We've dealt with children going to residential care, emotional meltdowns, investigations (both from DCS and the police), health issues and more.

Often times we're asked how in the world we keep going. We understand where this question comes from. It comes from a place of security. This world bases the success of life on whether you're secure, have enough material possessions, the right job, the perfect house, or the fairytale storyline. This isn't what we base our worth on as a family. We base our worth on relationships. We measure our success in the tiny steps forward as we walk alongside our children. Our family story is one of redemption.

We have so many tremendous blessings from adopting. Here are just a few:

Others

Adoption has a way of bringing people together. You meet a lot of interesting and amazing people through the adoption journey. Before long, others join your circle and your community grows. This is one of our favorite parts of being an adoptive family. When we've least expected it, we meet others who are on this journey.

Adoption has expanded our territory as human beings. As we were wrapping up this book we had one of those expansion moments. We were in Seattle speaking at an adoption conference. During the second night, we were both tired and were looking at ducking out early, grabbing a bite to eat, and crashing big time in our hotel room. We are from the midwest so the time change was a killer.

As we left the auditorium, I (Mike) happened to notice that they were serving free Q'doba for dinner. It was free…and it was Q'doba. These kinds of amazing alignment of the stars in the heavens don't happen all that often so we had to take advantage. We both decided that we would grab a table in the back of the dining area, eat quickly, and escape before anyone could talk to us. I'm glad our plans failed.

A few minutes into eating, another couple asked if they could sit with us. We instantly struck up a conversation, shared a little bit about ourselves, and connected over our mutual stories. Minutes later, another couple, joined us. *Two hours* later we finally left the room because the janitors turned the lights off on us! We felt as though we had been with people we had known for years. The conversation was deep, authentic, raw, and honest. In the weeks since, we've exchanged text messages, funny videos, encouragement and prayer. That's the amazing power of connection through the adoption journey.

Small Victories

Often, when you've been on the journey for a while, it's hard to see very far into the future. You start to question if this journey is worth it because the pain and struggle are so great.

We measure our success in the small victories. A detached child, who has gone for years without so much as a handshake, finally throws themselves in our arms and gives the biggest hug possible. A son who pursues everyone else but me finally calls me daddy. The emotionally dependent child finally decides to go into his Sunday school class without tears or tantrums.

Celebrate the small victories as they come. They are blessings. When you reach one small goal you will have the hope and the strength to reach for the next.

Health

Watching your children go from unhealthy to healthy is one of the biggest blessings you can receive through adoption. When our third oldest daughter first came into our care, her hair was a reddish color from malnourishment and she couldn't say a complete sentence. I remember driving her to her pre-school and saying over and over again, as she conversed with me, "I don't understand what you are saying honey." She would become really frustrated with me. With time and a healthy diet her hair became a beautiful dark brown. With consistency and a lot of speech therapy, and she learned to not only speak properly but also find her own voice. At 14 years old she is smart, funny, and beautiful. I am overwhelmed as I look at her and think about how far she's come.

Future

Adoption is about shaping and re-shaping the future. It's about changing the life of a child who otherwise might not have had an opportunity to succeed in this world. It's about allowing your own future to become something bigger than you ever dreamed of.

CHAPTER 22

The Power Of Community

We are passionate about creating support communities. Our support community has pulled us out of the most hellish moments, encouraged us when we were struggling, and surrounded us when we felt isolated, alone and defeated. The adoption journey can be a very long and lonely journey at times. For the first couple of years of our adoption and foster care journey we didn't have the kind of support we do now. We pretty much trudged along, hoping to find our way.

That changed in 2011. We had adopted through the foster care system, so we were invited to take advantage of post-adoptive services such as support groups and training sessions. To be honest, we resisted because we had been through some unpleasant experiences before. We would show up and they would share with us all of the ways we were failing as parents. "We don't need anyone to tell us that!" we both thought. The group we were invited to was a last ditch effort on our part. We were going through a really difficult time with one of our sons. We half-heartedly decided to give it a try. We loaded all of our kids up in our van, and headed for downtown Indianapolis. At the very least, they offered free food.

Once we got all of our children settled in we made our way up to the conference room and took our places in the plush, high back chairs. No one spoke and no one looked up at anyone else. This was as awkward as it could get. We found out later that everyone else in the room was thinking the same thing that we were- "We don't want to be here. We are overwhelmed. We don't need anyone to tell us we're failing!"

After several minutes the facilitator entered the room and kicked things off. She welcomed us, shared that this was a safe place, and then asked us to go around the table and tell our stories. For the next hour we listened to couple after couple share their struggles, heartache, pain, hurts, fears, and failures as a parent. Everyone had adopted their children through the foster care system and had the open wounds to show for it. It was as if each person rolled up their sleeves to show their gapping wounds. The most amazing part of the meeting came from the facilitator. As each person shared their honest story, she just nodded. Occasionally she would say, "I know. That's hard. I know how much that hurts!"

That night we walked out of that room feeling alive...because we realized we weren't alone. There were others who had wounds like us and were limping through life as we were. It was empowering. There's something healing in finding out you're not alone.

Building a Support Community

How do you form community? How do you find people who can help you, challenge you, but also understand where you're coming from. How do you decide who's a part of that community, and who isn't?

The first answer we usually give is this:

Not everyone will be in your support community. You don't want everyone in your inner-circle because not everyone belongs there.

When we adopted our first daughter people gushed all over us. They would say things like, "Awe, you guys are such saints for taking in a little girl who wasn't yours," They would remark on how wonderful and giving they thought we were for choosing adoption. We learned pretty quickly that these people, while nice and friendly and loving, did not belong in our support system.

People who gush all over you, see you from a distance but not close up. They say things like "You're a saint," or "God bless you for doing this, you're amazing," Their amazement and kind words may be genuine but they cannot remove themselves from an outsider's perspective. They can't see our children for who they really are. They don't value our children or view us as a real family. Their seemingly kind words do more to damage the validity of our family than they realize.

Our support community consists of families who "get it." They have familiarity with adoption. They do not see us as unique. They just see us as a family. Our support community holds us accountable, understands our struggles and loves our children and us unconditionally. They speak truth. They love us through our ugliness and heartbreak. They never flinch when we're falling apart or our kid is completely out of control.

One of our closest friends came to help during one of our son's rages. It had been going on for hours. We had enacted our safety plan, which included locking our other children in a room for their own safety. This friend walked along side me (Kristin) as our son continued to threaten, curse and rage. My friend stepped between me and my son as I wrestled a 12x12 paver out of his hands. In the process, he dropped it on her foot. Once the ordeal was over, she went on to spend the rest of her evening in the emergency room. She has seen the harsh reality of raising a child affected by trauma but she does not back off. She does not hide from us. She shares this life with us. She loves our son as she loves a nephew. She "gets it."

You need people in your support community who....

1. **Get it!** You want people who clearly understand the adoption journey and why you chose to go on it. Your greatest support will most likely be families with similar stories.
2. **Are non-judgmental.** God gave you the child you were meant to raise. He entrusted you with this responsibility. You know your child better than anyone. Do not allow judgmental people into your circle.

3. **In the trenches**. Look for families in your community who have similar stories to your own. Find people who have children with the same special needs. For one of our daughters adopted at birth, her biggest struggle is not knowing her birth family. She does not have any special needs, she does not have a tragic back-story, but her feelings of loss are real. She gains support from another little girl who has a similar story. The shared story makes each of them feel less alone.

4. **Point.** This one always raises some eyebrows until I take the time to explain. This does not mean including people who point at you or make a spectacle out of your family (as if I needed to explain this! :-)). Lord knows all of us who have adopted, or fostered-to-adopt, have been a spectacle more times than we can count. What this means is that you want people in your support community who can point you to healthier places. In your thought process, in your actions, with your emotions, and with your understanding. Adoption is hard. In fact, the hard days will most likely outnumber the easy days. This is a fact. You will inevitably have days, or weeks, or even months where you come unglued, meltdown, or feel like quitting. In these irrational moments you need a person, or people who can point you to a healthier place. This should never be a person who agrees with you on everything, nor should this be a person who lacks the capacity, or confidence, to challenge you or question you. It should be someone who loves you unconditionally, is trustworthy, has a clear picture of what this entire journey is like, and is willing to call you out and push you to think, feel, and act differently.

How do you decide who makes the cut? Our answer is- You interview them. Test the waters with your story. Share certain parts of your story, openly, with people. Then, observe their reaction. Listen to how they respond. Watch how they react. Do you have anything in common? Do you feel refreshed after talking with them? Is your relationship reciprocal? Do you pour into them as they pour into you? You will build this community in the same way you build any friendship. With time and patience. You will be able to loosen your boundaries a little at a time and let relationships grow.

The Power Of "Together!"

Once you've found people who get it, and won't judge you when you fall apart, it's time to start living life, knowing that there are people in your corner, even on the darkest days, and through the darkest moments.

"I can't do this crap anymore!" I (Mike) said, glaring at the table, with clinched teeth. My friend John agreed. Many colorful words were exchanged between us, that morning, as we sat talking in a restaurant. The steam from our coffee snaked and twisted through the air, disappearing, as if hope was slowly disappearing from our lives. We shared similar wounds. Both of us had children adopted from foster care and both of us were in very dark and desperate situations.

My kid routinely used his floor as a toilet just to "show us," while his son had begun threatening to kill kids at school. This was only the tip of the iceberg. There we were: broken, desperate, hopeless, but together.

Together. There's something powerful about that word. Say it to yourself: **Together.** It kind of fills you up, doesn't it? The road of adoption and foster care is filled with brokenness, despair and a lot of hopeless days. Let's just call this journey what it often is- _lonely!_ *Alone, isolated, and misunderstood* is a pretty desperate place to be...

The Desperation Of *Alone.*

For the first few years of our foster care journey, we were alone. We didn't know any other foster parents. We felt we couldn't share our struggles with anyone.

Say these statements to yourself....

- I deal with my child's traumatic past.
- I suffer the scars of my child's repeated rejection.
- I feel my child's special needs are a reflection of me.
- I walk the road of my daughter's severe reactive attachment disorder.
- I hide away from the neighbors while our son throws violent tantrums, screams obscenities, and destroys our house.
- I cover my bruises and scratches from my child's physical assaults.
- I spend hours trying to help my son do homework that his brain cannot understand.
- I rarely sleep because my 2 year old wakes up from nightmares.
- I am exhausted.
- I bear the brunt of my daughter's rage.

...you've felt the loneliness and isolation from each, haven't you? You're not alone...

Together IS Powerful.

This road can be long and scary but there is power in traveling together.

Together. It's a game-changer! It's a hope-builder! Say those same statements from above, again, but this time, place the word "together" in front of each:

- *Together....*we deal with our child's traumatic past.
- *Together...*we suffer the scars of our child's repeated rejection.
- *Together...*we come to the understanding that our child's special need has nothing to do with us.
- *Together...*we walk the road of our daughter's severe reactive attachment disorder.

- *Together*...we face the neighbors while our son throws violent tantrums, screams obscenities, and destroys our house.
- *Together*...we uncover our wounds and begin to heal.
- *Together*...we find resources to help our son learn.
- *Together*...we lean on one another in-spite of our sleepless nights.
- *Together*...we rarely sleep, but *together* we get a cup of coffee and trudge through the day, a little less exhausted than the last.
- *Together*...we bear the brunt of our daughter's rage.

Together. Not alone. Never hopeless. Always supported, held up, held together, loved, and understood!

That morning, John and I walked out of that restaurant empowered. Not problem free, but empowered. We knew beyond a shadow of a doubt that we were in this fight together. And because of the power of together, we would make it to the next day, and the day after that. *Together.*

You Are Not Alone

The most powerful part of discovering *"together,"* is that you are no longer alone. You have companions on this journey- those who can stand in the gap for you when you are ready to give up. Those who can sit and cry with you.

My friend John and I, will often text back and forth in the middle of the day. We'll text about vacation plans, getting our families together, our kids having sleep overs, the hilarious thing the DJ said on the morning radio show, and life's frustrations.

The other day John's text reminded me just how powerful it is to find out you're not alone. You see, our families are very much the same. Both of us are adoptive parents, both of us have been foster parents, and both of us have children with special needs. We are walking the same road. Our children struggle with the same things. We deal with the same weariness and stress as parents. His two daughters and two of mine are homeschooled.

We each have a daughter who slacks off with her school work, or ignores assignments altogether. It has almost pushed our wives over the edge.

I shared my frustration with John, and frankly, I was embarrassed. I shouldn't have been though. His text back filled me with strength.

"No man. We are in this together. Homeschooling can be hard on our wives."

A text like that is so simple. Just a simple declaration of solidarity. We could read a book, download a podcast, watch a Dr. Phil episode (or not!). We could see a specialist for ADHD or a counselor. We could consult with a psychologist or a psychiatrist. Finding those resources may be helpful, but they come up short. The outside resources lack Hope! At the end of the day, the author of the book is not in our home. Dr. Phil is a celebrity. The specialist locks his or her office, gets in their car and drives to their house, not ours. The psychologist shuts his computer down. The psychiatrist leaves to get her nails done. They're all helpful, but they fall short of hopeful.

Finding someone real, who also lives this life, adds a glimmer of hope. There's nothing more healing! There is something powerful, something healing in simply finding out you're not alone.

Finding Hope.

The other day my wife had a conversation with an acquaintance that opened up about her son's stay in a psychiatric wing of a local hospital. As my wife listened to her heart she identified. Our son has stayed in the same unit in the past. We've walked through the secondary trauma of a child who's completely out of control, violent, and destructive. My wife knew each tear dripping from her eyes.

While she couldn't offer any solutions, she could say from her heart, "You're not alone!"

As you journey through the ups and downs of adoption, or foster care, we want you to know you are not alone. We rejoice with you and weep with you. We are in the trenches with you and we know all about the wounds you've sustained. But we also know the heartbeat within your chest that keeps you going, even when all seems bleak. We have the same heartbeat in ours. We started the adoption process all those years ago, because we believed in a dream. We wanted to change the lives of children. Still do!

May you keep going, keep believing, and keep loving the children you've been blessed to raise and lead. And may you know that you are not alone on this journey!

RESOURCES

Over the past 13 years we have worked with many wonderful people, and met tons of people whom we consider family. These are the soldiers of the adoption journey, working hard to create forever families, and be the support when the journey gets tough. It is our pleasure to share the contact information for these amazing organizations. May you find the same blessing and hope through them that we have!

i. **AdoptUSKids-** AdoptUSKids.org
ii. **The Adoption Support Center-** adoptionsupportcenter.com
iii. **Bethany Christian Services-** bethany.org
iv. **Show Hope-** ShowHope.org
v. **Empowered To Connect-** EmpoweredToConnect.org
vi. **The Refresh Conference-** TheRefreshConference.org
vii. **No FAS-** nofas.org
viii. **NTI Upstream-** ntiupstream.com
ix. **Christian Alliance For Orphans-** ChristianAllianceForOrphans.org

ABOUT THE AUTHORS

Mike and Kristin Berry have a passion for reaching adoptive and foster parents with a message of hope and healing. They are the parents of 8 children, all of whom are adopted. In their 13 years on the adoption journey they have had the distinct privilege of parenting every age group of children (from birth to young adult). Their blog, confessionsofanadoptiveparent.com has been read by more than 2.5 million people all over the world since it's beginning in 2012. If you're in the Indianapolis, Indiana area, drop them a note. They would love to sit down over a cup of coffee and talk about adoption, foster care, being on the struggle bus of parenting, their favorite Girl Scout cookies, why they think controlled burns that fire departments do on abandoned homes are the best thing ever, or just life in general!

HOW TO CONTACT MIKE AND KRISTIN-

- Mike's email- mike@confessionsmail.com
- Kristin's email- kristin@confessionsmail.com
- Blog- confessionsofanadoptiveparent.com
- Mike's Twitter- twitter.com/itsmikeberry
- Kristin's Twitter- twitter.com/kristinsberry